HOW TO RISE ABOVE ONESELF *TRANSCEND!*

Theodore C. Kent

University Press of America,® Inc.
Lanham · New York · Oxford

Copyright © 2002 by
Theodore C. Kent

University Press of America,® Inc.
4720 Boston Way
Lanham, Maryland 20706
UPA Acquisitions Department (301) 459-3366

12 Hid's Copse Rd.
Cumnor Hill, Oxford OX2 9JJ

All rights reserved
Printed in the United States of America
British Library Cataloging in Publication Information Available

Library of Congress Cataloging-in-Publication Data

Kent, Theodore C.
How to rise above oneself : transcend! / Theodore C. Kent.
  p. cm
Includes bibliographical references and index.
1. Self-actualization (Psychology).

BF637.S4 K455 2002   158.1—dc21   2001056885 CIP

ISBN 0-7618-2185-6 (pbk. : alk. paper)

∞™ The paper used in this publication meets the minimum
requirements of American National Standard for Information
Sciences—Permanence of Paper for Printed Library Materials,
ANSI Z39.48—1984

DEDICATION

I dedicate this book to Robert O'Connell, a retired business executive, who on reading the manuscript insisted that I send the material in for publication to benefit others. After writing and rewriting it many times I found myself discouraged with it and put it away. On his advice I returned to work on it. I will quote Albert Schweitzer: "At times our own light goes out and is rekindled by a spark from another person. Each of us has cause to think with deep gratitude of those who have lighted the flame within us."

Contents

ACKNOWLEDGMENTS vii

PREFACE ix

Chapter 1: How Can One Rise Above Oneself? 1

Chapter 2: What Does "Transcend" Really Mean? 11

Chapter 3: Three People Who Transcended 19

Chapter 4: Adventures in Trying to Transcend 31

Chapter 5: Transcending Divorce and
    Our Two Human Natures 41

Chapter 6: How to Transcend Pain 51

Chapter 7: How to Transcend Temptation 61

Chapter 8: When Will We Rise Above Ourselves? 69

Chapter 9: Creative Evolution
    is the Key to Transcending 81

Chapter 10: Transcending or Psychotherapy,
What is the Difference? 95

Chapter 11: Topics for Discussion 103

POSTSCRIPT: THE ORIGIN OF HUMAN GOODNESS 115

BIBLIOGRAPHY 121

INDEX 123

ABOUT THE AUTHOR 127

Acknowledgments

I first wish to acknowledge the contribution made by Robert J. O'Connell to whom I dedicated this book. He was very enthusiastic when he read some of the notes I had made on how to transcend which I did not intend to publish. Later he made the index for this book. I give a special thanks to Dr. Robert P. Hopkins, a friend, neighbor, and psychologist, who encouraged me to start and then to finish this book.

As usual in my career as an author, my wife worked hard to smooth out some of the sentences in the book and did excellent proofreading. This time we were also helped by our friend, Shirley Slater, who applied her proofreading skills to every chapter and Helene O'Connell who helped organize the index and also did proofreading of the manuscript. I thank Joe Hamilton for his dedicated work in keeping my computer and printer operating in spite of their temperamental desires not to cooperate with me. It seemed as if the subject of "human goodness" threatened them.

PREFACE

"How does one rise above oneself?" The title of this book does not refer to levitation that might be performed in a magic show when a beautiful woman, at the magician's command, mysteriously rises into the air and floats above the stage. However the reader may find it even more miraculous that it can be accomplished in another way, that is by transcending.

What does it mean to transcend and what does it entail? The purpose of this book is to explain this so that the reader can understand and be able to utilize the "magic." Transcending hate, envy, revenge, and other destructive emotions in order to be able to reach a higher self may convey to some the idea that this is a spiritual experience more appropriate for saints or mystics rather than for ordinary people. Those who think this are mistaken.

This book will attempt to demonstrate that the ability to transcend does not require sainthood but, rather, a clear understanding of what is involved. Many people who regularly use the word, "transcend," have only a vague idea of what it means. Actually, instead, I shall show that the word can have a number of other interpretations that may confuse people. Because they lack an understanding of what is involved in transcending, many people spend their lives living in a box of narrow thinking instead of reaching into the broad, open spaces of their minds as being able to transcend would enable them to do.

I intend to describe steps that readers can take to emerge from the narrowness of their emotional lives. If properly understood, transcending is an extraordinary human experience because it reawakens the idealism that may have existed earlier in a person's life. Idealism tends to make transcending a unique experience and differs it from psychotherapy. This difference can cause misunderstandings that place obstacles in the way of achieving transcending. Neither is transcending exactly a religious experience. For example, the ability to forgive is a great human accomplishment. Rightfully, it plays a large role in religious values. Transcending has nothing in common with forgiving as used in a religious sense. One can transcend only that which happens to oneself. It is a lonely experience.

The mystique in transcending stems, in part, from the fact that, when it is most needed it occasionally occurs instantaneously and without the effort of the person who transcends. Instantaneous occurrences like lightning and thunderbolts as well as sudden insights inspire awe. However, unlike some therapeutic flashes of insight, transcending does not lead to a sudden recognition of one's shortcomings and subsequent regrets. As this book will show, transcending occurs within a different dimension from many other human experiences.

Finally, readers of my book are entitled to know that transcending is not appropriate for all the conditions we may encounter. Some of these we must endure. Nevertheless, transcending will help us gain a new perspective. In spite of the fact that it may not solve every problem, the word "miracle" comes closest to describing the new way we may feel about ourselves after we have learned when and how to transcend. Then we may gain a new outlook on ourselves and the world around us.

Theodore C. Kent, Ph.D., Sc.D.
Ventura, California

CHAPTER ONE

HOW CAN ONE RISE ABOVE ONESELF?

At some time in our lives most of us confront seemingly insoluble problems that stir up negative and angry emotions within us. As we struggle to cope with these feelings someone may advise us to "transcend" them. Transcend means "rise above them." How can one rise above one's own feeling? Clear instructions on how to transcend seldom accompany this advice.

Rising above oneself is difficult to imagine. That is why it is hard to obtain an explanation of how to transcend that one can actually apply. The word may even bring thoughts of jumping through spiritual hoops or engaging in some kinds of mental contortions. Some people view transcending as related to mysticism, meditation, or as a branch of psychotherapy. It is none of these. Those who try to describe what to transcend entails often fail to offer sufficient details to enable anyone to achieve it. This is unfortunate since we could probably override some of life's most painful experiences if we knew how to successfully transcend them. Then we would be able to deal more easily with other events in our lives.

Why do some people with emotional problems refuse to turn to psychology (the science of the mind) to help them find their way out of their troubles? Richard E. Johnson, a successful psychotherapist (who served as the director of clinical training at the University of Regina, Canada) has an answer. He was the author of the book, *The Quest Of A New Psychology,* (1975), in which he wrote:

> My own rejection of psychology ... stems from years of professional work as a psychotherapist. I have discovered from those countless hours of critical human experience that man is something much more profound than a complex animal or a machine.

This is a point of view which an increasing number of psychologists hold. In Chapter Five of this book the reader will find a reference to another psychologist, Sigmund Koch, who had a similar view of psychology as that of Johnson's. In the year 2001, the journal, *The American Psychologist* (May, 2001) contained five articles which discussed Koch's criticisms of modern psychology. Transcending meets some of the objections that have surfaced and yet I will not condemn the good work that psychologists have done and will continue to do. Some of the difficulties that we face today exist because we are human beings who live in our modern world. Later chapters delve into some causes of our contemporary discontent.

More than a half a century ago, Karl Menninger, (1942) of the Menninger Clinic wrote:

> ...no one will maintain today that all's right with the world. It is full of hate and murder and bitterness and hunger and waste and pessimism and fear and sorrow.

It is difficult for people to achieve inner peace in the kind of world which Menninger described. Nevertheless, it is the kind of civilization in which we live today. Some wonder if any well-intentioned person can be content with current human behavior after reading our newspapers or watching our television. Nevertheless, it is possible for us to achieve inner peace by transcending. Once we have learned to rise over and above that which disturbs us, we can set an example that will contribute towards making our world better for ourselves and others. The motivation "for others" represents the idealism inherent in transcending. This is where T therapy (T = transcending) differs from psychotherapy.

I was a successful psychotherapist for many years. However, in some way I was dissatisfied with myself. I had the feeling that the teaching of psychotherapy as it was practiced lacked something. At that time I was not sure what it was. I wished to learn more about human beings before continuing. I went back to a university for a second doctorate in a different field, anthropology, in order to broaden what I could offer my clients. I found later that what I was looking for may have been idealism. Contrary to the definition of psychotherapy, transcending must be an idealistic process. That meant our happiness must contribute, in some way, to others as well as to ourselves.

It is important that first we must understand that "rising above something" does not mean to ignore it or to be indifferent to it. The fact is that we can be in touch with two of our human natures. "Rising above" occurs within ourselves when we leave the dominance of the first of these human natures for guidance from the second one. In a previous book, *A Psychologist Answers Your Question,* (1987) I mentioned that when we leave one of our human natures and go to the other one we are taking the longest trip a human being can travel. In actual space, however, it consists of merely going from our lower brain center to the higher one in our cerebral cortex where our prefrontal lobe is located. It houses our inhibitions and good judgment. In that sense, we have a higher self within us that this book will describe. It is most easily reached by seeking the larger picture of a situation. The larger picture is the one that enables us to look beyond the details that, at first, bombard our senses and capture our attention when things go wrong for us. This larger picture gives us a sense of responsibility towards humankind and even to the universe. That thought is not too difficult to grasp. It is actually more difficult to imagine that we humans, singly or together, remain unconnected to anything else.

We have the capability to look at a larger picture of almost any situation. Whenever we do this, a sense of obligation toward our fellow humans may arise within us which is not distracted by hostile thoughts or desires. That sense of obligation manifests itself increasingly with all attempts to transcend. In short, transcending evokes a feeling of concern regarding what happens to people other than ourselves. The results help to create an improvement in human relations that could be obtained through the use of psychotherapy as well as through transcending. However, there is no inherent need for psychotherapy to be humanistic. In contrast, it is built in to be so in transcending.

Transcending has as its distinguishing characteristic that it is rooted and guided by a practical kind of idealism. It is literally able to "hop over" annoying and troubling events and yet take note of them and ascertain their cause. This creates a kind of idealism which does not have the identical academic meanings of "idealism" described in some philosophical textbooks. Idealists are not merely the opposites of realists as some may suppose. The idealists to whom I refer are those who feel, at least a small measure of *desire,* to make the world better than Dr. Menninger described it. They feel this to the extent that their position in life enables them to successfully do so. Not every idealist transcends, but all those who are able to transcend have some measure of common-sense idealism which guides them to reach what I have called their "second human nature."

In my years of teaching I have found the concept of a first and second human nature helpful in explaining applied behavioral science to college students. The idea of a first and second human nature, as I use it in this book, has no exact similarity to

Freud's concept of ego and superego. Contrary to Freud's view, the second human nature can be seen as anatomical and genetic as the first is, rather than solely the result of environmental exposure.

Today a sizeable amount of the idealism which every normal person is capable of experiencing is blocked from our vision because we are frequently exposed to human brutality in the newspapers and on television. Just knowing that this exists creates in some of us a dissatisfaction which most of us have learned not to admit. This kind of a dissatisfaction was mentioned by the American author, Henry David Thoreau who lamented it when he wrote the often quoted words: "The mass of men lead lives of quiet desperation." (*Walden*, 1854). Note the fact that the desperation was described as "quiet." It is so quiet that most people are hardly aware of it until one day some of them look into their mirrors and realize that they feel worthless and unfulfilled. This doesn't happen to everyone since we have had a lifetime of cultural experience in masking this aspect of living.

The ongoing dissatisfaction of many people to which Thoreau alluded prompts some to search out books on self-improvement. Retail bookstore shelves abound with such self-help books. Some of these books offer their readers helpful hints on how to live life more skillfully and with more satisfaction. However, a sizeable number of readers of such books find the results of their reading disappointing. Some people cannot follow the instruction for achieving their goals. Others are unable to make the changes in their life-styles that these books recommend. In contrast, people who transcend do not need to turn themselves inside-out. Their common-sense idealism is a natural human attribute that has evolved through creative evolution which I will describe in later chapters. I plan to convince the reader that the idealism to which I refer is available to all those who seek it. And, it can also be exciting.

We shall describe later that there are many important ways that creative evolution differs from biological evolution. Unfortunately, idealism can be aborted and shriveled up by the blows people receive in living their lives. However, people can restore their idealism and expand their focus to include a "bigger picture" in which idealism can again become meaningful. People who have learned how to transcend, recapture their idealism by drawing again upon a power that they have within themselves. As I have already mentioned, a second human nature — a creative one — is available to them if they reach up for it and rise to meet it. How to accomplish this is described later.

As we shall see, transcending usually cannot be learned by employing the techniques or methodologies of psychotherapists. In transcending, people need not seek an altered state of consciousness as in meditation, yoga, psychotherapy, hypnosis or, not to omit them — the mind-altering drugs. They need only to rediscover what they already have — their own second nature which I shall describe in some detail in the next two chapters. Then they will be able to re-evaluate their lives and find a motivation for idealism that they failed to discover in themselves before. It is not surprising that many individuals who have eagerly sought to transcend have failed. They have looked for the keys to success in the wrong places. They did not realize that successful transcending is rooted in idealism which they could adopt if they knew how to do so.

However, I must advise the reader that the road that leads to transcending may have some unsettling characteristics. For some people it may create a temporary sense of dislocation. When the discomfort of this experience has passed, as it will, these same characteristics lend transcending its power to heal. Those who transcend must discard their familiar small picture view of the world as Menninger described it in the beginning of this chapter. They must fit their thoughts into a big picture that is humanity-oriented rather than purely self-oriented as is psychotherapy. They will find that after learning how to transcend, they are able to profoundly change their interpretation of what they encounter. The Greek poet and playwright, Aristophanes had something to say about this as far back as 450 B.C. He wrote:

> From the murmur and subtlety with which we vex each other give us rest. Make a new beginning. And mingle again the kindred of the nations in the alchemy of love. And with the finer essence of forbearance, temper our minds.

This illustrates the idealism that is present in our human species as a *potentiality* upon which we can draw for our use. To be able to apply it we must rise above ourselves in the way that individuals who have accomplished this are described in the chapters that follow.

Before I leave this chapter, I will give an example of "above oneself" as it may occur in real life. Some years ago while taking a walk I caught up with a man in our neighborhood who, like myself, was walking for his health. As he joined me we talked. He told me that recently he had undergone major heart surgery. When he first heard his diagnosis he said that he was stunned by the bad news but what surprised him most was that as time went by he began to consider his medical ordeal as a blessing.

"It took me out of my self-preoccupation," he confided, "and made me aware of the larger world that I had never bothered to really look at before." Not until his near-death medical experience had he appreciated the warmth of his family. He found comfort in their love of which he had not been as keenly aware. "Before I had my heart attack I was always preoccupied with things that happened to me personally. Now that I have had a heart attack I realize that in the big picture view of my life the things I worried about were largely inconsequential."

His experience had led him to look *beyond* himself and take a big picture view of his life. It taught him how to rise above his former self and to transcend. Each time there is a favorable mutation among living creatures they also are able to rise above their former selves. This is typical of those who discover idealism within themselves which they had not been aware existed. There is nothing complicated about discovering one's own idealism. It does not require heart surgery to accomplish it. One person I once interviewed summed it up in just two sentences as follows: "I found that I am not as important as I had thought I was. I realized that other people were more important than I had thought they were." This contradicts the concept that the most important activity for humans consists of spreading their genes as far and wide as they possibly can. This is seen as "successful" survival according to the theory of biological evolution. This is not in accord with transcending therapy. There will be more on the subject of human goals later in the book.

I shall summarize what I have said thus far. The crux of transcending is found in somehow rising above one's instincts and primitive emotions. This is accomplished by realizing that every small picture has a bigger picture of which the small picture is only a part. The larger the picture view one envisions, the further the horizon expands. For example, in the sky there may be a single cloud above our heads. If we focused only on the cloud we might say, "the sky is cloudy." However, if we look at the entire sky we would get the impression that the sky is blue and mostly clear. The small picture view would have given us the wrong impression because we did not look *beyond* or *above* it. This is also true when we look at ourselves. In our busy life we are apt to obtain a mere glimpse of something or of someone and then view and label the entire event or person by what we initially focused on. Without an awareness of what "beyond" or "above" is we will never discover our true inner strength. This is because "beyond" and "above" reveal a whole different world in which everyone who wishes to transcend becomes partially immersed. It will enable us to rise above ourselves.

Chapter Two will give us a picture of how to transcend from a historical point of view that will offer us an additional insight into what to transcend entails. Chapter Two will help to view some examples of how to transcend described in Chapter Three. As we shall see, these occurred to people like us.

Chapter Two

What Does "Transcend" Really Mean?

Now let us look at how dictionaries define "transcend" and contrast it with how it will be used in this book. We shall discover that in the evolution of the word there were several meanings which explain how it became tied to idealism. This bit of history of transcending will help us later to understand why it is such a marvelous activity.

Dictionaries define transcend, as "to rise above or go beyond the limits of something." The Latin word *transcendere* means to climb through or across. I find this interesting, but it is too literal a translation to convey all that is involved. The title of this book implies that we are able to rise above the part of us that interferes with the satisfactions in our lives. If we took dictionary definitions literally, we would fail to get any notion of the current meaning of transcending. Unabridged dictionary definitions of transcend include such descriptions as "overpass, surmount, exceed in excellence, outdo in some attribute like quality or power." Transcend, is illustrated in dictionaries in phrases as "the tale of adventure transcends belief," "the grandeur of Niagara Falls transcends description," "his love of people transcended national boundaries," "Cleopatra's beauty transcended all others." Theological meanings include, "to go beyond material existence." These phrases by themselves do not offer us the kind of picture we need to comprehend the word in its larger sense as we apply in this book.

Let us look further at the related words, "transcendent," "transcendental," "transcendentalism." These have different emphases but share a common root with transcend. The ancient Greek philosopher, Aristotle, saw "transcendental" as something beyond any category of things known to humans. Some 18th century philosophers agreed and described the meaning of transcend as mentally going beyond the limits of all experience and knowledge. This they claimed, could only be achieved by going above and beyond something — which comes close to how we use the word in this book. However, it was the American poet, Ralph Waldo Emerson, who saw "transcending" as an activity that involved inspiration and idealism. We, also, see "inspiration" and "idealism" as essential words that describe the most important aspect of "transcend."

Some time ago, I was asked to write a description of people who transcend. I wrote, "they are persons whose bright new vision of the world emerges out of the fog and confusion in which they previously attempted to understand their lives." This is because such persons are given new eyes to see beyond what they failed to see before. As their eyes move from a small picture view to a larger one encompassing it, they penetrate the world of appearances and reach the essences which make up the larger world. Essences are often elicited by asking, "Why?" Appearances on the other hand more often describe "How?" or "What?" People who have learned to transcend often ask themselves "Why?" Their answer may be the very heart of idealism. For example, on Christmas many people pray for peace between all nations. As they reflect they may ask "Why do people have to hate each other? What has hate accomplished for our species?" In their attempt to answer these questions they may think about the history of our species and reach the conclusion, "I favor world peace but there is just so much I can control." Many people regret that we must curb some of our idealism in order to accept the world as it is. Transcending opens up the opportunity to escape from this dilemma. This is not an easy thing to do. For this reason we have a habitual need to change ourselves. Changing our appearance is an easy way to begin. It is a characteristic which may have been among the first of human efforts.

The large number of references and the diverse descriptions of changing ourselves from human beings into something else must be signs of human longing for the experience. This longing takes on a new significance in an age of genetic engineering and cloning which we are now entering. Our species' romance with changing ourselves is reflected in body manifestations which appear in the legends of many cultures. We reveal this in wearing clothing even when clothing is not necessary to keep us warm. Tattooing is found world-wide. Some pre-Columbian Meso-Americans artificially elongated the shape of their skulls to conform to the concepts of the local fashions of their time. We can take an example from *Revelations*. We have the following (12-1): "And there appeared a great wonder in heaven; a woman clothed with the sun, and the moon under her feet, and upon her head there was a crown of twelve stars." This word-picture represents the woman transcending her earth-bound existence to attain cosmic dimensions where all things are one. It describes the widespread universal human longing that optimists, like the author, believe in some future age may lead humans to have a family feeling toward each other. This would greatly reduce the numbers of murders and wars that occur world-wide today. There are people now living who have suffered through periods of unbelievable cruelty because other humans refused to accept them as fellow human beings. Dehumanizing others becomes a permit to treat them with cruelty and serves as a license to kill them. It is the tool of terrorists and we must understand this tool if we wish to create a safer world.

When I read the description of the woman in the sky from Revelations to my five year old granddaughter, she had no difficulty visualizing the scenario. Her comment was, "Of course, grandpa, the woman was an astronaut!" In a sense my granddaughter was right. Long before we reached out towards the sky utilizing airborne rockets, we did it symbolically in our minds by visualizing a larger picture for humans than those that were confined to earth. We might say that all those who transcend are "astronauts." They have reached a higher ground above themselves. These, like the vision of the woman clothed in garments of the sun are a wonder that occurs right in our midst, here on earth. They are the people who transcend and find that life can be different in a world of big pictures instead of the everyday small ones that are constantly called to our attention.

In the teachings of Buddha, the first of the four rules he prescribed for his disciples was that they must wear old and cast-off garments in order to avoid the material values of the world. However, people often misinterpret a religious leader's teachings because these leaders use their second human nature which is not easily understood by their followers. There was a letter to the editor in a recent *National Geographic* magazine from a writer in Florida who pointed this out. I quote his letter below:

> Poor old Buddha. Spurning his vast family inheritance, he lived a life of asceticism and worldly deprivation — teaching his followers to eschew all prideful things of the Earth. Now, while millions of their countrymen are starving to death, some Indian Buddhists are building a hundred thousand dollar gold statue in his honor! They have no idea of what he died attempting to teach them.

We know that the same fate applies to other great religious leaders.

Another story tells of a Buddhist priest who found himself attracted to a pretty woman who flirted with him to test his resolve. He struggled against her attraction until he forced himself to focus his total attention on her white teeth. This brought the image of a skeleton's white bones to his mind and enabled him to resist her advances and turn away. His self-control was restored because his idealism had prompted him to accept an ascetic way of life. Let us take note of the fact that religious sacrifices lean towards abandoning aspects of our first human nature. Sometimes mental associations, as the one made by the monk, are helpful in transcending and rising above some of the instinctive impulses from our first human nature. Such mental associations are like crutches that help us walk upright when we are too weak to do so without them.

As I have said before, we have two human natures. When we transcend, we rise above our first human nature in order to reach our second one. Our first human nature is physiological, instinctive, self-protecting, and self-centered. It ranges from crudeness and utter selfishness at its lowest point to a more tolerant form of "it won't cost me anything." Because of our youth as a species we listen to our first human nature most of the time. Without even thinking we obey its dictates most of our life. These include sex, hunger, thirst, and physical security. It harbors impulses to get even for slights and insults. In contrast, our second human nature is often silent. It may not manifest itself to us until we actively look for it. As I have stated before, specific life circumstances often make us aware of its presence. It is founded on resolve and a reflection of the higher priorities in human life. It reaches out to others and to the world with modesty, compassion and good will. It points us to the direction which we hope humanity is headed and from which it is likely we shall turn away if we regress.

I have found it sufficient to refer to the two human natures we have within ourselves, a first and the second one with the qualities I have described above. Other psychologists may suggest that more than two human natures exist but I feel two natures suffice to explain our need to understand the capabilities of our lives.

Our two human natures seem to give us something like "split personalities." Even those who transcend sometimes shuttle between them. This enables us to be kind and caring as well as, at different times and circumstances, indifferent to other people's suffering. Sometimes persons, under the sway of their first human nature, would scarcely recognize themselves under the influence of their second human nature and vice-versa. "Was this really me?" they may ask themselves incredulously after reflecting on what they did or thought. Nothing could make less sense to someone totally under the sway of his first human nature than the exhortation, "Love your enemies and pray for those who persecute you." Our first human nature would say loudly and clearly, "Punish thine enemy to stop him from tormenting you again, or better still, kill your enemy in order to get rid of him!" To love someone who has hurt you is difficult for almost anyone. In order to merely tolerate such a person we must reach above ourselves.

This brings me to a recent newspaper article that illustrates my point. It was headlined, "A Sniper at Peace With His Duties." It describes how a Marine sniper was noted for his skill in being able to kill dozens of people at one time during the war in Vietnam. After his return to the USA, he became a forest ranger. He received attention for risking his own life to save other people's lives during forest fires. The newspaper article reported that when his role in Vietnam was revealed to those who knew him as a life-saver they were stunned. "It just didn't compute," said a friend. "He is such a low-keyed and nice guy that people couldn't believe that he was capable of his earlier killing during the war."

We are all capable of doing things that seem incredible to us when we are prompted by our two different human natures and, later, reflect upon what we did. It explains the insightful biblical saying, "let not thy left hand know what thy right hand doeth." Some of the anxieties from which many people suffer today may stem from the conflicting messages sent us from our two incompatible human natures. To extricate themselves from such dilemmas people may allow their first, self-centered nature to pretend it speaks for their second, humanitarian one. It explains much of the hypocrisy philosophers find exists in many urban societies since ancient times. The resulting pretense, however, is usually not of long duration since our first human nature is apt to take measures to identify itself with a "see what I did!" bravado. Then the excuses pile up in our minds and most of us end up thinking of ourselves as pretty nice guys after all.

Thoughtful people know that life can be an extended learning opportunity, and if they are so inclined, they can learn something new every day. What they may not be aware of is that all learning is a way of transcending. It closely follows the definition for transcending I have given. From the first chapter the reader will recall that transcending requires us to take ourselves *beyond* something else to reveal a bigger picture of the world. This is a way we can rise above the common annoyances that confront us.

No matter how much or little we may use it, all new learning takes us beyond the previous boundaries of our life experiences. Our first human nature constantly fears that it may lose control of us and, therefore, it persuades us not to apply any new learning to the way we act. As we know our first human nature is possessive. After all, it saw us first and it tries to keep us ignorant of our second human nature that could compete with it. The lives of people who use only their first human nature is one of unhappy marriages, poor relationships with their colleagues, and an ongoing lack of satisfaction with those around them. They often experience a self-hate that is puzzling to them since they think of themselves as good, honest, hard-working citizens.

However, an understanding of our second human nature is required to inform us about the concepts that are usually involved in transcending. Examples of the use of our two human natures will surface throughout the book. These examples will help us to further explain what "transcend" is all about. Much of the mystery and hazards of being a person who transcends will appear in the next chapter. Also there will be illustrations and guidelines that will help to teach us how to transcend.

Chapter Three

Three People Who Transcended

To be able to transcend we must have two goals. One is to improve our own life so that we can live more fully and gain peace of mind. The other is born of idealism. The idealism I use in this book can be described simply as a wish to leave the world as a little better place than we found it. In other words, to try to make a positive difference in our lifetime. These two goals mutually reinforce each other since those who wish to create good relationships among people are likely to improve their own lives. Not long ago I read a statement that I think is worth repeating: "Caring people have a wonderful way of making a difference in the lives they touch." I add, "including their own." Those who wish to transcend rudeness or even wrongs done to themselves, realize that they can either perpetuate or transcend such behavior. A headline appeared recently on a front page article in our local newspaper. It read, "Professor's Philosophy of Life Unshaken By Stabbing." An explanation followed.

> The professor in a small California college was stabbed twice in his chest by a mentally disturbed student who used a six inch knife. The student was a 22-year-old man who had a previous history of mental problems.

The stabbing was not a retaliation since the student had passed all of his classes this semester. He was walking towards his dormitory when the professor recognized him as he drove by and offered him a ride home. The student accepted it but became increasingly agitated when the professor chose a route unfamiliar to the student. The student took out a six inch hunting knife from his knapsack and without warning stabbed the professor twice.

The professor was able to accept this attack as an act of a disturbed person and did not hold it against his student. While the professor was recuperating in the hospital, the parents of the student visited him and tearfully apologized for their son's action and asked for his forgiveness. "Of course!" the professor assured them, "I have been lying here trying to figure out how to reestablish a therapeutic relationship with your son." Needless to say that the parents were greatly relieved.

It is important for us to be aware that persons who transcend a wrong committed against themselves do not thereby abandon their ethics or moral behavior. Jesus did not encourage cheek slapping by giving instructions to turn the other cheek after one cheek had been slapped. This should be kept in mind by those who read the examples of transcending in this chapter. Neither did the professor encourage stabbing by transcending the actions by the mentally ill student. We can only transcend wrongs committed against ourselves and hope that the way we react to them may discourage the wrongs from being repeated against others. These hopes represent the idealism that is part of the transcending picture.

One thing we can expect when we attempt to transcend is that whenever we experience wrongs (or imagined wrongs), our response from our first human nature will be quick and strong. It usually is accompanied by an outpouring of adrenalin and a rise in blood pressure. That is why it is helpful to have our second human nature — the one we use when we transcend —

ready to respond to a new situation. As a species, we humans suffer from an evolutionary lag in maturity when our psychological perception encounters any hostility from others. We tend to exaggerate it in our minds. Because we have a great need to receive love from our fellow humans, hostility by members of our own species threatens us with extraordinary severity. That is why our most dangerous enemy is not an angry tiger but a hostile member of our own species. In order to create a better world, persons who transcend acting with revenge for wrongs committed against themselves, are the kind of persons that the world needs today and has needed since ancient times. The reader should keep this in mind as he reads the examples that follow later in this chapter.

Let us also recall that I have tried to caution the reader that transcending has limitations. For example, transcending would not be suitable for use in legal matters where justice must be the rule. Civilization would crumble if people transcended actions committed against the law. We must always remember that to transcend is a lonely experience and that it must remain an act available to individuals who choose it of their own free will. In a way, that gives it a kind of glamour because it is a rare example of free choice.

Let us now note the emotions involved in a real life situation when transcending takes place. All the examples that follow are from records of actual clients I interviewed while I was a therapist. We shall begin with the description of a very difficult task of transcending. The situation strongly called for the first human nature to get involved. Yet transcending required the second human nature to guide the person who transcended.

EXAMPLE 1

On a single lane road a person drove his car past the car ahead of him forcing that driver to swerve off the road in order to avoid an accident. I shall refer to that driver of the car forced off the road as the "victim."

Common Reactions

The first human nature of the victim would be called up immediately and 1) The victim would be outraged at the other driver. 2) At the same time he would experience feelings of relief that a near-accident had been avoided. 3) This might be followed by an angry impulse from the victim's first human nature urging him to push the other driver, who caused the near-accident, off the road or to actually strike him. Now let us compare these feelings with the reaction of one who wants to transcend the episode.

A person who wants to transcend: 1) At first, a person who wants to transcend might instinctively react like anyone else — that is, with a rise in blood pressure as he swerved to avoid an accident. He would initially feel anger at the person who caused the near-accident. 2) A short time later, the person who wishes to transcend would experience his second human nature and would move beyond the event. Instead of anger he could focus on his luck in having avoided what might have been a serious accident. 3) At this point, the person who is trying to transcend would deliberately dismiss all impulses to "get even" and might, instead, speculate on why the other driver took such a risk. 4) He would attempt to comprehend what could have caused the other driver to act in such an aggressive manner. 5) Now, instead of merely wishing to condemn the dangerous driver for causing the near-accident, the victim would like to help him be able to avoid his dangerous behavior in the future. Thus, the person who transcends is prompted by his idealism to look *beyond* his near-accident and, instead, to envision a larger picture of possible future casualties that might be caused by this driver. Then he might try to lessen the chances of similar danger caused by the driver. He might conclude that a report to the police would be the best way to prevent similar future accidents. Without rancor or desire for revenge, he would call the police to report what had occurred. Primarily now, the mind of the person who transcended, was focused on the possibility of danger to others.

From the previous description we realize that transcending is facilitated by at least an average intelligence. The victim might have realized that the other driver could have been either emotionally unstable or under the influence of alcohol or drugs, or just a very angry person and for any of these reasons would have been a dangerous driver. Thoughts of this kind help a victim to consider things beyond the deed itself. Introspection helps to involve the victim's second human nature as well as his intellect. Thoughts that question other persons' state of mind typically help any victim to transcend. That worked for the monk, I described in Chapter Two, when he concentrated on the flirtatious woman's teeth to remind himself of her skeleton after her death and of his vows of celibacy. This helped him to allow his second human nature to take over.

Transcending usually follows a pattern: 1. Something or someone did something that hurt you. 2. Remembering your goal to transcend prompts you to respond without anger or hate in return. 3. You call on your second human nature to envision the big picture view which takes you beyond the event and weakens your initial reaction. With practice (or because of circumstances) the big picture view could then come to your mind even without your conscious effort; 4. Once your second human nature is fully involved, intelligence and idealism can further guide your behavior. You may shake your head in wonder at things that can happen in our world but you do not do so in anger.

Some people are helped to reach this goal through the use of highly respected role models whose behavior they wish to emulate — Buddha, Lao Tze, Jesus, Gandhi, Schweitzer, Martin Luther King Jr., or others who have traveled this road. When you are able to transcend you may become a role model to others. If we follow the examples of others whose morality we admire, or if we ourselves are used as an example, we shall experience a deep satisfaction because this is how we shall know that our life has made a positive difference. In my book, *Genetic Engineering, Yes, No, or Maybe* (2000) in the chapter in which I compared Jesus' life to that of Nietzsche's, I pointed out that Nietzsche admired control over others while Jesus taught that control over self is a much greater accomplishment. We know that this requires the use of our second human nature.

EXAMPLE 2

Let us take a totally different example of transcending. A working class couple unexpectedly inherited a large sum of money from a distant and almost forgotten relative. Thereafter, husband and wife and their two small children moved into a gracious upperclass neighborhood. The houses there were large and the whole area was composed of well-tended estates. In the above scenario the family found that they were not welcomed by their neighbors. Instead, they were looked down upon by the majority of the people living in this exclusive suburb. The newcomers could understand why they were not accepted. Understanding is often a first step in transcending because it implies looking at the larger picture of a situation. The new couple were determined to transcend the indifference and, at times, the hostility they encountered. The wife greeted her neighbors with an agreeable smile even though it was rarely acknowledged. She did not attempt to break through the social barriers but remained cheerful in spite of the fact that she could not interact with her neighbors.

When neighbors walked past her with their eyes averted she focused her mind on their common humanity. At first this was not easy. But she knew that her neighbors were responding to her with the same human nature that she also possessed but chose not to use. This helped her avoid both pain and anger. "There but for the grace of God go I," she would sometimes mutter to herself as they passed her with their noses in the air. She pictured herself doing to others what they were doing to her and told herself that she was not a better person than they were. She was determined not to become angry at them for rejecting her. She found that her previous experience in meditating, which she had practiced occasionally, helped her to awaken her second human nature.

In spite, of their neighbors' unfriendliness, the couple were always ready to help the neighborhood and the school with various projects. In time some of their neighbors realized that the newcomers were good people in spite of their obvious lack of some of the advantages that the others had. Although months passed before their neighbors would acknowledge them as "one of us," in time it happened. Meanwhile, in the school yard, the couple's two children went through the usual "test-teasing" as had all other children new to the neighborhood. Soon the couple's two children were accepted by their peers and played well with the other children at the playground. No transcending was necessary. A lower or higher social class does not matter much to young children.

A change came about with time and many in the neighborhood began to respond to the couple in a friendly way. Some of them actually became the couple's close friends. The couple was able to handle their initial rejection because they understood its cause and did not try to retaliate. Their idealism in this situation, kept them from bitterness and feeling resentful. Their big picture view was, "We are all God's children." Their focus was on turning the other cheek.

I do not say that idealists never get angry. Idealists are capable of becoming very angry in the face of injustice to others. But, as I stated at the beginning of this chapter, those who wish to transcend try to respond to the big picture view of those who irritate them. By looking at the big picture view of a situation, the couple were able to call upon their second human nature and could live in peace with their neighbors, in spite of their initial rejection. It is well to remember that the first human nature of a person usually attracts the first human nature of others and that the second human nature also tends to respond to the second human nature of other people. Although it takes time, using their second human nature is one way that those who transcend help to make it a better world. If more of us used our second human nature when interacting with our fellow human beings, perhaps, we could then attain the elusive world peace for which so many of us long for. However, we leave this speculation to a later chapter. This brings me to the third example.

Example 3

Newspapers recently reported a story of an African-American man who had been falsely imprisoned for eighteen years. The so-called witnesses to his alleged murder of another man had mistaken him for someone else. He was freed after a group of lawyers who were interested in his case, proved beyond doubt that a different man had been responsible for the crime with which he had been charged. Later, when confronted, the actual murderer confessed. Upon his release reporters asked the wrongly imprisoned man how he had been able to handle the injustice he had suffered for eighteen years. He gave a two word answer which was reported in the newspaper, "I transcended."

The former prisoner had been sentenced to life in jail. How could a person in his circumstances have transcended an entire lifetime in prison? What could his larger picture be? What could have called up his second human nature? How, in his false imprisonment, could he have found any idealism? Transcending has been called, "crossing over or above an event to reach the other human side." In the case of the man accused of murder, some felt that the "other side" could only have been his execution. When he explained that he had transcended, did that mean that he had looked forward to death? If he had to die for a crime he did not commit, would his big picture view have to be, "The world is unfair?" He avoided such questions because he was able to turn to his religion in order to obtain his big picture. Religion can often be the "big picture" for many people because it offers them comfort. There are also other ways that do not involve religion with which to see unhappy situations in larger perspectives. One of these is to keep up one's hope for justice and that those who were mistaken see their errors in the end.

The former prisoner explained, "God knew I was a victim — not a murderer." Thus his big picture view was, "God knew that I was innocent." In his own mind his belief that God knew of his innocence, helped him transcend the painful experiences of his confinement. At the beginning of his jail sentence he was bitter — as could be expected. As time went on, he concentrated on thinking about the people of all races and religions who, since the beginning of human history, had also been wrongly accused. Somehow this helped him feel that he was not alone. He bonded to these unknown people and found comfort in viewing all innocent victims of unfair treatment as his soul-mates. While still in jail he mentally shared his bad luck with them and found a semblance of companionship which further helped him achieve peace of mind in spite of his false imprisonment.

FURTHER DISCUSSION

When, later, I had the privilege of interviewing the man who had been falsely imprisoned, he explained that while in jail he had focused on each single day, instead of taking a long view of his life. This was the opposite approach to looking for a "big picture" which I previously have recommended. Awareness of only a very much shortened portion of the picture is a time distortion that under some circumstances can be helpful. The former prisoner said that by thinking only from day to day, he cut his sentence of life-in-prison into only 24 hours at a time. Time distortion — mentally arranging time to be most suitable to one's peace of mind — can be used as a form of transcending. It is another way to move "beyond" or "behind" an event. It helped the falsely accused prisoner to accept the prison routine and allowed him some freedom of thought without having to experience a daily, ongoing bitterness. He told me that after he began to transcend his prison life, it had much less of an emotional impact on him. The initially hated prison routine became almost meaningless. Finally he visualized it simply as a nuisance like someone forced to live in a narrow house with inconvenient furnishing. The question that most of us would be likely to want to ask him is, "Where under these circumstances could a person falsely imprisoned find idealism?"

His answer to this question convinced me that the capacity for finding idealism even under difficult circumstances is built into most human beings. Most of us can find it if we earnestly search for it. We find it if we discover traces of our own second human nature within us. Some find it through meditation. Others may catch sight of it during illness, or through suffering, or victimization, or near death experiences. Many people conceive of something they view as "spiritual" at various times during their lives. The man who had been falsely imprisoned told me during my interview with him that he had found his idealism in his faith in God. This did not permit him to give up all hope for justice. He believed that the laws of his country, as a whole, were meant to be just. He accepted the fact that in his case a terrible mistake had been made and that the majority of the people in the world would agree with him. Among the big pictures that helped to sustain him in his small jail cell was, he told me, that justice was, nevertheless, the goal of the law. This thought and his religion took him beyond the prison walls and helped him to transcend his life in prison.

We should note that the ex-prisoner never had outside guidance in how to transcend. His only alternatives were great bitterness and despair. He wanted very much to avoid these. As so often happens, necessity was his teacher. After he had thought things over, he learned how to use the prompting of his second human nature. In my interview with him after he was released, I asked him how he had learned to transcend. He replied honestly, "I don't know." He had discovered his second human nature without having been aware of how he did it. I have mentioned a combination of things that helped him. My interview with him revealed that his false imprisonment left no deep emotional scars and that he was unlike others who had experienced injustice and who remained bitter and vengeful throughout the rest of their lives. He had no severe post-traumatic symptoms after his release. This he was able to accomplish because he had transcended.

Later this man was invited to speak on transcending at the local Boys' Club and invited me to accompany him. He told the boys "Always remain yourself. Don't let anyone else make you into somebody you would not respect." The former prisoner continued, "That is exactly what the desire for revenge and anger will do to you. Shake off such thoughts as the wish to get even or pay back someone who has tried to hurt you. Rise above it. You will then not allow others to determine for you what kind of a person you will be. This will greatly help you to live a happy life in which you can maintain your self-respect."

I could see the look of admiration on many of the boys' faces. This did not include all of them — but I expected that. The satisfaction on the face of the former prisoner was easy for me to see. It made me think of how it is still possible to teach many young persons, who are at an impressionable age, to become good people. It gives me hope for our human future.

Chapter Four

Adventures in Trying to Transcend

It is interesting to learn that it is possible to transcend without being aware that we are doing it. This could happen when we try to save ourselves from worrying or becoming aggravated. However, awareness of what we are doing could bring a touch of adventure or even a bit of humor to the situation. To seek to transcend consciously and retain awareness of it, gives you the advantage that you can prepare yourself for it. Preparation is often necessary.

To illustrate this point, I shall tell you about Fred with whom my wife and I often had dinner. It was over the dinner table that he told us an interesting medical episode he had recently experienced. He explained that he had been scheduled for cataract surgery which had been arranged several weeks in advance. We had talked about the benefit of transcending and he planned to try to transcend the physical discomfort of the surgery. He recalled that transcending required him to discover the big picture of a situation. He did this by focusing his mind on the expectation of improved eyesight. He chose this as the big picture on which he would concentrate. He had anticipated that he would not be able to drive himself home after his surgery and had arranged for transportation.

When Fred arrived at the hospital on the day of his scheduled surgery he was somewhat surprised that he was told to get completely undressed and lie down on a gurney. He was given a sheet and told to cover himself with it. He didn't expect that eye surgery would require this. As he lay under the sheet in the hospital, a young man in hospital attire asked him for an authorization card from his health maintenance organization which authorized the surgery. He had no idea that he would be required to present such a document at the time of his surgery. Since he was unable to produce the required card he was told to get dressed and reschedule the operation later when he could produce written authorization on another day. Given that request, his second human nature took flight and left him alone with his first human nature. As a consequence of this, his first human nature provided him with all of his long-forgotten curse words which he now mumbled quietly to himself.

To avoid further anger, Fred again determined to transcend the new situation that he now faced. He wanted to keep anger out of his life as much as possible. In order to do this, he searched for a big picture view of his present situation, but hard as he tried, he couldn't think of one. Instead, all that came to his mind was that the hospital was in need of a total revision of its scheduling system. As he looked at himself draped in a sheet, the situation suddenly appeared terribly funny to him. Laughter came to Fred's rescue. As he got dressed, he continued to chuckle at his predicament.

I asked what made him laugh. He waited a moment and then answered, with a wink, "the thought of telling you about this experience and asking you how you would have handled it. How would you have transcended it?" he asked looking straight at me.

I had to think for a moment before I could come up with a reply. At last, thankful that I had thought of a way out, I answered, "I'd try to imagine *you* under the cover of the sheet and the expression on your face when you were told to get dressed and to make another appointment."

My answer made him look seriously at me and ask, "Is laughter at oneself a legitimate way to transcend?" He knew that I was in the process of writing a book on the subject. "It worked for you, didn't it?" I replied. "Since it worked, accept it," I suggested.

When everything else fails, the use of humor is still a good way to transcend. Laughing at oneself is a way of overcoming frustrations, and it implies that you have sensed a bigger picture in the background. It makes you go beyond your first human nature to see yourself in a new light. That creates an adventure in transcending.

Another adventure of a different type appears when you interact with someone who speaks with a double meaning. Actually, transcending cannot take place when people say things to each other that have double meanings. This is especially true if a person is aware of only one of his or her meanings. Then, often some detective work may become necessary. One way to handle that is to transcend the person's spoken words since they do not express his meaning. This is not usually desirable since it can break the bonds of a relationship. The best thing one might do under these circumstances is to try to be aware that a double meaning exists. We should be aware that double meanings complicate the task of transcending. Obviously, before transcending can take place, one must identify what is to be transcended. One cannot see beyond it or leap over it if the object to be transcended is unknown. The question, "What are you trying to tell me?" may be difficult to answer because the individual himself or herself doesn't know what he or she really intends to communicate. Anger can be disguised or hidden so that it remains unrecognized. The expression of the anger may be "catharsis" which, in psychoanalytic terms, means, "to relieve one's tensions by giving them expression." The word goes back to the Greeks where it meant, "to heighten the effect of a drama on the audience." The presence of catharsis can sometimes be recognized when a person's words and acts contradict each other.

Sometimes what people say to each other has a double meaning. The problem is that often the people who say the things with double meanings are aware of only one of their meanings. This complicates the task of transcending. It is very important to be aware of what one wants to transcend. As I said previously, "What are you trying to tell me?" may be difficult to answer because the person doesn't know what he or she really means, and worse — *he or she doesn't know that they don't know it.* When this is called to any person's attention, bad feelings almost always erupt. Those who speak with two different meanings — one, perhaps, for tension reduction — and the other to communicate something else — are usually unaware of it. Therefore, under some circumstances, it may be wise to avoid calling attention to the fact that a person has given you something that has a double meaning. A person who intends to transcend must, however, be alert to the occurrence of this fairly widespread human tendency. For example, "I am right," often actually means, "I am a good person." The minds of people who say, "I am right" and mean, "I am a good person," often become hopelessly entangled so that one thought stands for the other. If that happens, even the smallest error made may mean "I'm a bad person." This can further be translated into "I'm not much good!"

If we accept this observation that I have made during years of psychotherapy, imagine how this impression of "I'm not much good" could be magnified if a person's belief involved some important subject. Within family situations, quarrels may start from what appears as nothing more than innocently doubting someone's "facts." The feelings turn more angry if someone demands that the person who presented the "facts" verify them with proof. This is more likely to happen in a family if both marriage partners insist on always being "right." Therefore, merely to attempt to correct someone's factual error, can sometimes precipitate an angry denial. I have found that there is nothing that is as vigorously defended as a doubtful fact or even an untruth. This is because it would too clearly rebound in the mind of the person who made the statement as, "I don't know what I'm doing — *therefore I am no good!*"

Let's consider the following (fictional but true to life) example of double meanings which I have put together from my psychotherapy experience.

Mary: "The weatherman on the television warned that it will rain today. Tim, better take your raincoat to the office."

Tim looks out of window and replies, "There's not a cloud in the sky, Mary, I very much doubt if it will rain."

Mary, "You can't tell by looking out of the window now whether it will rain this afternoon."

Tim, glancing through the morning newspaper at the table, "I see nothing in the paper that predicts rain, Mary. Are you sure you heard right that rain is predicted?" "I heard it very clearly, Tim," and so on. The situation often ends with some bad feelings.

Their anger intensifies when Tim comes home soaking wet. Mary greets him with an aggrieved voice, "Come in and get some dry clothes on, Tim. Next time, listen to your wife!"

Tim's response is a growl. "You always have to be right!" he mutters to himself as he stalks off to put on dry clothes.

In the above bit of drama, the rain had nothing to do with the cause of the misunderstanding. Let us see what might have happened had it not rained. Tim would have come home and said, "See, it didn't rain, Mary. Either you didn't hear it right or the television weatherman on the TV was mistaken as he so often is." Mary might feel anger that Tim now was unfair to the TV weatherman and this made her think that Tim was additionally unfair to her, too. Similar hostile feelings may be aroused among spouses when communications are expressed in gestures and not directly in words. Sometimes angry feelings are not expressed at all. They are held within and internalized creating a psychosocial distance between married people who wonder why their love for each other has disappeared.

Neither Tim nor Mary were aware of the fact that they were talking about something totally different than, "Will it rain?" They were talking about, "Am I right?" which has the deeper meaning of "Am I a good person?" Had Tim and Mary known what they were *really* talking about, Tim might have taken his raincoat, folded it, kissed his wife goodby that morning, or Mary may have said nothing about rain as Tim left for his office. In other words, they would have avoided the question of "Will it rain? or "Who's right?"

One of my students coined a phrase for doing this. She said it is using "deliberate, salutary absentmindedness," which she viewed as an emergency way of transcending the untranscendable. Transcending cannot be "forced" into situations from which there is no hope of extricating itself. The student was right. To respond with silence may be viewed as a form of transcending which has, from time to time, been used by some very wise people. They have learned that when things get too complicated, "Silence is golden" and therein lies wisdom. Nevertheless, as we shall learn later, with young people of school age, this highlights a job to be done. It is to acquaint them with some practical aspects of using human nature two or some other means of redirecting their anger. The horrible alternative, exemplified by one fifteen-year-old, mild-mannered boy shooting and killing his High School classmates when he no longer could tolerate being teased by them, must not continue.

It is interesting that after the above paragraph was written, I received a copy of my November 2000 *Journal of Psychological Science* with an article by Joel Weinberger, Ph.D. on misinterpreting the teaching of the psychologist, William James (1842-1910). The author of the article wrote:

> Distortions of an individual's views is not unique to William James. Great historical figures are often co-opted to support currently popular positions, through selective and out-of-context quotations. For example, Thomas Jefferson has been invoked by both left and right to support and oppose almost every political important point of view in U.S. history. This is a dangerous enterprise. It allows us to put ideas that these individuals never had into their minds.

I will add that this "dangerous enterprise" appears to a certain extent in almost every household in which I have been asked to provide marital counseling. It affects the family's children. I estimate that as high as 60% of the usual family quarrels could be avoided if more married couples realized that "I am right," at a deeper level, often means, "I am a good person," and conversely, "You are wrong," could mean "You are a bad person." That is why "I am right," has, at times, been so ferociously defended by both nations and individuals. Unfortunately, religious people who feel singled out to defend God are sometimes examples of this tendency. Family quarrels have been successfully transcended by people who have applied my student's "deliberate, salutary absentmindedness" which kept them from becoming angry with each other.

Many marriages break up needlessly because of misunderstandings between two people who both speak the same language but whose words have different meanings. As far as communicating with each other, they may as well be speaking in a foreign language which only one of them understands. A former student in one of my Behavioral Science classes at the University of Southern Colorado visited me one day. During our chat he mentioned that he had recovered from an illness which left him with a loss of a good portion of his ability to hear. He was using an amplifier to hear to me during his visit. He wanted me to know that he felt that transcending was useful to anyone who had suffered a hearing loss. "Never did I realize how much of what we say to each other isn't listened to," he told me. "If I'll say, 'that's interesting' every now and then my popularity increases. Could the inability to hear be a form of transcending?" "No" I told the student, "but listening in silence to others may be thought of that way."

Recognition that a situation may not be as important as one thinks at the time of its occurrence may also serve as a form of transcending. My older sister, Margaret, was a clinical social worker who at times would remind me that whatever was upsetting me probably wasn't as important as I had first thought. I found that just thinking that it might not be so important could be very calming. Often there may be a very good reason why a situation which once seemed very important, is not as important as one thought at the time it occurred. An example comes to my mind. One day I lost my wallet with my credit card in it. Actually, I was sure it had been stolen out of my pocket while I stood in line in a drugstore to get some medicine. The loss of my credit card upset me very much.

I went home to borrow the money from my sister. She calmly asked how much I needed. "This isn't really so important," she said when she saw how upset I was. I notified my credit company by phone still feeling upset until they assured me that I would only be liable for fifty dollars of the total amount of charges incurred by the thief. This turned out to have been more than $2000.00. Later, I realized that I had slipped involuntarily into my human nature number one during this episode. When I still later read about an earthquake that had killed over a thousand people in India, I felt ashamed. I realized, as I had before, how easy it is to let one's first human nature guide one when one is upset. I also realized the wisdom of thinking, "it isn't so very important," when only limited amounts of money are lost versus people getting hurt or killed.

"Use more of your second human nature!" I told myself as all of us must occasionally. It taught me something I would like to share. It was the sad fact that no matter how much one knows about transcending, unless one is a saint, there is a good chance that one may slip back and follow one's first human nature some of the time.

This experience made me realize that a person who wishes to be a peacemaker must be aware of his or her limitations — especially in domestic quarrels. The hostility in such quarrels may have accumulated until they reached a bursting point. It could happen that by trying to create peace, a would-be peacemaker may find himself or herself at the center of everybody's anger and be blamed for everything that is wrong. Intelligent knowledge of one's limitations may be seen as a real accomplishment of transcending. Likewise, acceptance of one's limitations, by itself, can bring with it a measure of peace of mind. It is well to be aware that one did not create all of the strife and chaos that exists in the world and that one is incapable of preventing most of it. Knowledge of one's limitations does not reduce a person's idealism. The motivation to improve the world can remain on an "I would if I could" basis. Obviously, the wish to be able to do it must be sincere.

Again I must caution the reader that transcending is a lonely experience. The advantage of this is that, since it is lonely no one can deprive another person of the peace of mind that it can bring about. And this can make transcending a very personal adventure for those who try to use it in their lives.

I was asked by some of my friends, who had read the high statistics of divorces occurring in the U.S.A., to say something in my book on transcending that might help divorced couples cope with their loss. When I found out the really large number of marriages that fail each year, I agreed. The next chapter's first part consists of a discussion on divorce.

Chapter Five

Transcending Divorce and Our Two Human Natures

Although a marriage may end, sometimes the former partners can retain mutual respect for each other, pick up the pieces, and go on with their lives. However, after the dissolution of a marriage, many who dreamt of living happily afterward have to deal with very painful post-divorce emotions. Some will view their divorce as "heart-breaking." They must divide their possessions, their assets, wedding presents, his and her family's heirlooms, their pets, and most traumatic of all, their children if there are youngsters in the family.

Among the questions that must be answered are, who will obtain the family car? Will the house be sold? Will the children stay together with the mother or father? Among arrangements that have to be made are child support, visitation rights, and so on, and so on. It is not unusual for those who divorce to become depressed and even lose much of their self-esteem. However, most of the time this is not easily admitted even to oneself. Divorce is a traumatic experience even when both partners realize that it is preferable to continuous bickering and ongoing anger that occurs in a dysfunctional relationship. It is not surprising that both partners may end up feeling bitter after a divorce and blame each other for the destruction of their dreams of a happy marriage. In most of the countries where there is freedom of choice of mates, almost every voluntary adult marriage is accompanied by happy dreams of the future. Fortunate are those who, under some circumstances, are able to transcend the things that might otherwise break up a marriage.

Previously I have pointed out that idealism is an important component of transcending. We shall have more to say about the role of idealism as it relates to transcending later in this chapter. Persons who lose their idealism lose themselves, and may never be able to find themselves again in the hubbub of their lives. That is why we must ask, "how can idealism play a role in a traumatic situation such as a divorce?" Couples who had looked forward to their marriage with an anticipation of happiness would be hard pressed to find anything idealistic about a divorce, beyond the opportunity to escape from the big mistake they think that they have made. Let us go back to the original meaning of the word, transcend, to search for an answer. First we may recall that to transcend literally means to "climb over and beyond an event or an obstacle." Thus, after a divorce, we must mentally climb over and beyond an unfortunate marriage and do our best to leave it behind us. If we have learned anything from the divorce which might be applied in the future, it may give us the hope of happier times ahead.

In order to transcend a divorce, or almost any traumatic experience, some find it helpful to think back and review their lives from as far back as they can remember. If this sounds like psychoanalysis, bear in mind that no analyst nor any other person need be involved and no new psychological insights need be gained. In transcending therapy, what is sought instead of insights, is a feeling of wholeness of self and self-togetherness. Some people may insist that insights can provide this feeling. However, in some cases this is true while in others, it is not. We can use mistakes that we have made in the past as a learning experience which will help us do things better in the future. An awareness of this can help us to bring the big picture of our life together and create within us a sense of wholeness which heals. Hope for a happier future is always a big picture for which we can search after a divorce. A divorce, or any other trauma in life will be remembered with less pain if we see a holistic picture of our lives and move beyond any point which was only one sad part of our life.

Those who wish to transcend the trauma of a divorce or any major disappointment must try to be fair and honest in their evaluations of themselves. This may not be an easy thing to do and they may need some help from others. Next, they must recognize and regret any mistakes they have made in their relationship and then they must forgive themselves for having made those mistakes. My experience has been that those who are unable to forgive themselves fail to see any measure of idealism within themselves. You may have to look for traces of your second human nature in order to find your idealism. Then you might be surprised when you discover it although you had never thought that it had been there.

In my clinical practice, at times I was able to convince my clients (by means of their own answers to a series of questions) that they were, at least partially or "vaguely" idealistic even if they preferred to see themselves as villains, as some did. Nevertheless, the fact that some had missed seeing the worthwhile side of themselves was a part of the reason that they were filled with dissatisfaction. It accounts (if I may again quote Thoreau as I did in Chapter One) for their "lives of quiet desperation."

THE ROLE OF IDEALISM

I have interviewed people who insisted that they had no need for idealism and did not believe that it was important in order to live their lives happily. Some even objected to the idea that idealism is a necessary part of transcending. In some respects they may be right but, as we stated in Chapter Two, we have chosen to select the poet, Ralph Waldo Emerson's definition of transcending in this book. Those who try to use idealism's principle, that all humans should be treated like one's brothers and sisters, may get badly hurt and disillusioned at times. This does not detract from its goal which is to create a kinder world for people and to help them feel better about themselves.

The world may not be ready for that kind of idealism as yet. However, such a goal is necessary for transcending to do its job to improve human relationships and distinguish it from Freudian "ego defenses." These can be used to avoid becoming upset with ourselves since they allow us to blame others for our troubles. Ego-defenses offer humankind an easy way out of their dilemmas. They help to avoid the bother of self-searching which, in turn, avoids self-blaming.

For those attempting to transcend there is even better news. In trying to transcend, merely *the attempt* to introduce idealism into one's life is already an indication of actually gaining a measure of idealism. Success in transcending begins by merely trying to do it. Trying, rather than succeeding, is also the measuring stick of gaining idealism. The change of heart that leads one to *try* to transcend implies a conversion of the mind. By itself alone, it represents a momentous accomplishment.

An important distinction between psychotherapy from what we may call "transcending therapy" now comes to light. Certain aspects of psychotherapy may work largely through our first human nature with instincts and self-protection as its primary focus. It is true that behavior can be "corrected" by some forms of psychotherapy as, for example, in behavioral therapy. Cognitive therapy requires us to understand what we are doing and why we are doing it. It is helpful since it is based on our understanding our problems from the start. Transcending involves largely our second human nature guided by idealism. Therefore it is directed at others as well as oneself. An important distinction between what we may call "transcending therapy" now comes to light. Certain aspects of psychotherapy may work largely through our first human nature with instincts and self-protection as its primary focus. Transcending, from the start, involves largely our second human nature guided by idealism. Therefore it is directed at improving the lives of others as well as one's own.

Perhaps that is the reason why, for some time, I have found something lacking in the study of psychology alone and therefore, also in the practice of psychotherapy. After living a lifetime wondering about this and thinking about transcending, at last I became aware of what was missing. I realized that success without idealism is not really success at all, when looked at from the large picture view of humankind. My "problem" had been that I wished to see the world from the large picture view of humankind. I learned from life itself, that life has to have some kind of purpose at its center to produce a true feeling of satisfaction. That may be because everything that happens in the universe in some way changes it. If we contribute to making these changes by the way we live (small as what we do may be), we help shape the universe and, at the same time, give our lives meaning. I saw this most clearly when I wrote a book of poetry I titled, "Poems for Living," (1995). I shall reproduce a shortened version of one poem that expresses this thought:

There Is Purpose In The World

Some people tell us that the world lacks purpose
"Life has evolved through blind chance" they say
Random mutations account for natural selection
Produced by adaptation to an ever changing earth.

> In their myopia they view "the selfish gene"
> As the supreme monarch of all things alive
> The single-minded monarch gives but this command -
> "Survive, increase, spread me across the earth!"
>
> Where is the scientific evidence of purpose?
> It lies unrecognized within that very question
> Purpose is found in asking who we are,
> Where are we going and what can we accomplish.
>
> With humankind a purpose for the world was born
> To banish random chance and replace it with justice
> And to rebel against the rule of selfish genes,
> To sing, and dance, to play, and to create beauty.

All those who believe that our job as human beings is "to banish random chance and replace it with justice" are idealists who give human lives a purpose. We should all be aware of the fact that idealism can sometimes be twisted around to appear as its exact opposite. For some of us idealism is a necessity, not a luxury. Neither college degrees, nor self-acquired knowledge, nor fun, nor sports, nor job success, nor money can provide a substitute for idealism. A substitute for idealism simply doesn't exist.

CHOICE IN THE USE OF HUMAN NATURES

And now we come to a strange characteristic of idealism and what I see as its partner — transcending. As I have stated previously, a major part of transcending consists of simply trying to do it. Total failure is impossible for all who sincerely try to think with more care of their fellow human beings and with less of themselves. Merely to try to gain the awareness that we have a choice of human natures may suffice to arouse our second human nature to participate in our lives. It is fortunate that while we try to transcend, our second human nature may wake up by itself to help us. However, the struggle we must sometimes go through to use it makes it clear that our first human nature does not wish to relinquish any of its control over us.

Further difficulty may arise when our two human natures attempt to speak for each other as they sometimes do. We should all be aware that our first human nature might disguise its voice. We may be thinking we are listening to our second human nature when actually, our first human nature is talking. That is why we often have to struggle in deciding how to respond to events that we would like to transcend. We can often recognize our first human nature because it wants to pay back what it gets in kind. That is, insult for insult; anger for anger; a slap in the face for a slap in the face. This impulse comes from our first human nature and is always accompanied by feeling "he/she/they deserve it. It's only right!" Our first human nature is devilishly convincing.

People who have had severe emotional shocks or brain damage tend to revert back to their first human nature even if they have successfully left it behind during a healthier portion of their lives. Then again, they will return to fighting fire with fire instead of with water. But even in such cases, sometimes their second human nature may reawaken and may surprise them by showing up at the last moment before they act. There will always be exceptions, and even great ups and downs in human values among us. At times they may stun us and may make us very pessimistic about human life.

However, this should not keep us from seeing the big picture. Hopefully, over time, we shall move into the direction where we will no longer wish to hate one another. We can accomplish this by using creative evolution which will take time to fully click into place. This should not discourage us as long as we are not impatient and are headed in the right direction.

The characteristics of creative evolution are kindness, sympathy, and compassion prompted by the thought that we are part of something bigger (more on this later in following chapters).

As we consider our human attributes, we should remember that we are only children in biological evolution. On a scale of all of life marked on the face of a clock, we entered the scene only two minutes before midnight. As our species matures into adulthood, we may be able to firmly say to ourselves, "I shouldn't do this" and understand why we are saying it. At that perhaps *distant* date, our human environment and heredity may further combine to insert our second human nature more firmly into our human psychological makeup. We cannot tell at this time whether this would require a mutation which would increase the metabolic activity of the human prefrontal cortex. It has the task of censoring our thoughts and impulses. However, even without that, our present willpower aided by our imagination may be able to accomplish it by the spread of our ability to transcend. Alternately, through the increase in social pathology, crime, terrorism, or war we may join other species that have disappeared from the earth. This would not come about because of a lack of the intelligence necessary to survive but because we use too much of our intelligence to devise weapons with which we can destroy each other. In order to survive, our species must say "no!" to thoughts of mutual destruction. We humans are great imitators of each other both in doing good works and bad. The bad imitations receive most of the attention of the media. However, in the imitations of good deeds lies our hope for a future better world.

Need I add that a certain amount of optimism about Homo sapiens sapiens will assist transcending to spread. I have never heard of a confirmed pessimist who could successfully transcend. It requires a bit of optimism. Our continuing hope for a united human species will eventually lead more of us to our second human nature. Then the majority of human beings will, at last, be free of the destructive impulses which we still have towards each other.

Chapter Six

How to Transcend Pain

Let us look closely at people who search for happiness even though they suffer from physical or emotional pain. What surprises us is that they are able to make peace with their disrupted lives and find happiness despite their hardship and pain. This happens when they have been able to call upon some aspects of their second human nature which are concerned with others rather than self. It helps them to transcend their physical and emotional problems.

We all know that physical and mental problems differ. But they are not necessarily entirely independent of each other. The idea of transcending implies that for some, something of greater significance lies beyond their pain. This idea may be very important to those who suffer from any kind of pain. We have the tendency to make chronic pain the entire picture of the world that we see and feel. Transcending requires us to go beyond that picture.

First we must take into account that pain and pleasure are guidelines to behavior. They have a decisive role in shaping the actions of humans and animals. Pain and pleasure offer a simplified guide to what we may expect from the way we live. People are apt to regret feeling pain. However, they should remember that those who are incapable of feeling pain are greatly handicapped because pain usually serves as a guide to health. An inability to feel pain may even affect their length of life. Chronic pain, however, may be extremely difficult to live with for many reasons *beyond* the actual experiencing of the pain itself. In order to obtain some relief from chronic pain, it is helpful if we know its causes. For example, pain, from childhood on, may have been associated with punishment. That applies to both mental and physical pain. When we do something wrong or if we use poor judgment, pain often results. Mental pain can be associated with guilt. Conversely, chronic pain can produce a deep sense of unfairness to the person who is pain's victim. "I don't deserve this!" people have said bitterly when they were referred to me by their physician for hypnosis or biofeedback to try to help alleviate their symptoms of pain.

There is another side to chronic pain — the reward side. Through the years, I have had at least a half dozen clients with chronic pain who used it as a crutch to obtain sympathy and attention. In each case, the reward helped outweigh the negative aspects of the pain. One drawback of this kind of a "reward" is that clients with chronic pain will not admit that with treatment their pain had lessened or ceased altogether. They were reluctant even to share this with their doctor when he asked them how they were feeling. They enjoyed their secondary gain of special attention and sympathy too much. Therefore, in chronic pain, as well as with other chronic symptoms, there are a variety of ways to lessen the impact on its victims. The annoyance caused by every irritation depends to some extent on the big picture a person views behind the scenes. It may also depend to some extent on which of a person's two human natures are used to interpret the situation. It takes ingenuity, stubbornness, and imagination to live in some kind of harmony with chronic pain.

The majority of patients who seek help for chronic pain are individuals with post-traumatic disorders caused by illnesses, accidents, injuries of various types, or with the disabilities often associated with aging. In my practice I have had some success with using hypnotherapy with chronic pain patients. However, this may sometimes be a long and drawn-out procedure. Therapists who deal with these patients may have a number of surprises occur in their practice as the following example demonstrates.

I shall never forget a woman, about 45 years of age who was referred to me for hypnosis by one of the many physicians she had consulted. She came to my office complaining that she had suffered from severe back aches day and night for seven years. In vain, she had been seen by a variety of physicians, chiropractors, and acupuncturists. None of them had been able to relieve her pain. She told me that currently she had to spend most of her time in bed unable to do even the simplest housekeeping. She left making her bed for her husband to do, as well as all the other household chores. She said that she was very unhappy because she had always enjoyed doing the housework and felt useless and inadequate since she could no longer do it. Nevertheless, to a psychologist as suspicious as I can be, a variety of secondary gains occurred to me which her pain may be providing for her. I tried hypnosis with her reluctantly and did it primarily because of her insistence.

I found that she went into a deep hypnosis with little preparation from me. During the hypnosis I merely informed her that her back pain had left her. After that I told her that at the count of five she would wake up and be free of pain. I counted to five slowly and did not expect any success. When I finished counting, she suddenly sprang out of her chair, crawled on her knees to the chair where I sat, and kissed my shoe-encased feet. She shouted, "I feel no pain! I feel no pain! For the first time in seven years I feel no pain!"

She looked ecstatic. I recall that I was more than a little disconcerted by her feet-kissing response. Gently, I lifted her up to her feet and pointed to the ceiling with my finger to indicate to her that perhaps a Higher Power, not I, deserved the credit for her seemingly miraculous recovery. Regretfully, I told her the bad news. It was that one session of hypnosis almost never had any long term success in the relief of pain. Further, I informed her that hypnoanalysis, psychotherapy or medications were usually necessary to achieve a more permanent result. Even then, if the pain were to be identified as psychosomatic, extensive counseling would most likely be required to relieve it. Unfortunately, I was right. The next day the patient phoned me and announced that her back pain had returned.

I mention this episode out of my past to illustrate the fact that chronic pain may be very difficult to eradicate in spite of unrealistic hopes of the people who are afflicted. Before medications can be prescribed, the presence of chronicity of pain must be established by a medical specialist, often by one in orthopedic medicine or in pain management. Only after a thorough medical examination should a patient accept the diagnosis of chronic pain. After that diagnosis, patients who seek to transcend their pain may try to combine imagination with transcending in their search for relief. In order to do this, patients are asked to draw on their imaginations to paint a larger picture in their mind than the one that their pain holds for them. This has the purpose to enable them to see their pain in a different light. In some cases it may even require a patient with chronic pain to create a fictional big picture.

The first step in this type of therapy is to mentally separate the pain from any type of imagined punishment. "The pain is not punishment!" one can repeat this to oneself until it really sinks in. The next step would be to disassociate the pain from the idea that one has had bad luck. "No, it is not bad luck" I would advise sufferers to tell themselves. "Then what is it?" they may ask. People who suffer from chronic pain owe it to themselves to have the physical cause of their chronic pain explained to them. Then they might be able to put the true medical explanation out of their minds and give themselves an alternative explanation drawn from their imaginations. This does not work for everyone but has proven to help some who later are able to bear their pain with much less difficulty. Initially, this method of pain reduction seems bizarre until we recall what Albert Einstein once said in a different context, "Imagination is more important than knowledge." It also applies to many aspects of medicine and psychology. The state of one's mind influences the brain's neurotransmitters that, under some circumstances, have powerful pain reduction capacities.

There are some people who permit themselves to imagine that they were hurt while saving someone's life — perhaps a child who now lives happily due to their intervention. This satisfies some and gives their pain a purpose. Because the scenario is only imagined, it will not work for everybody. Others may have to be reminded of something they are apt to forget — behind the pain felt today there stands their whole past life with many past moments that were not associated with pain. Some people can enjoy these in retrospect. Besides their pain, it is likely that they experience some happy events even while they are in pain. They should concentrate on these which may consist of receiving some precious love from special people. And, if they are religious, they may feel that God loves them and they can pray that He will help them bear their pain.

Prayer and hope help many of those who without them would succumb to severe depression because of their chronic pain. On the other hand, there also are people who actually have trained themselves to appreciate a kind of paradoxical enjoyment of their pain. One person told me that he bore his pain stoically by imagining that he had committed a great crime and that his chronic pain was only light punishment for what, in his imagination, he actually deserved. However, this would also permit guilt to enter the picture of his life and, therefore, I only mentioned it but do not necessarily recommend it.

After visiting a severely disabled friend in a hospital, a person who suffered from chronic pain realized that things actually could be much worse for him than they were. He was able to compare his own situation with that of his friend who was, at the time of his visit, confined to a hospital bed. His own "big picture" that he referred to for pain management became the life of his friend in the hospital. One way to transcend pain is not to permit it to become the big picture in one's life.

A recent survey supports what I have already stated earlier in this chapter. What people who suffer from continuous pain find most disturbing is that they feel that they don't deserve the punishment that their chronic pain inflicts on them. "Why me?" is a common complaint. To be treated fairly is a universal human longing. We are reminded of the falsely blamed and imprisoned person described in Chapter Three. In his identification with himself he included all others who were falsely imprisoned and obtained solace from the fact that he was not alone. They were his "companions" in suffering. Some patients who attend group therapy sessions find that their suffering is reduced when they share it with others who are also suffering. Unfortunately, there are only a limited number of group therapy opportunities for chronic pain sufferers. To be of help there should be many more.

There are "heroes" who endure chronic pain without complaining. They view themselves as courageous. Some pride themselves because they don't mention their pain to anyone other than their doctor. It seems that their reticence greatly boosts their self-image. In their own minds they see themselves as superior. However, they are the exceptions who are able to more or less ignore their chronic pain. More frequently persons who suffer from chronic pain search for someone who is likely to give them sympathy and understanding. After they find a person who seems to understand what it is like to have to live with chronic pain they bear their pain more stoically.

A young man who suffered from chronic pain after a severe automobile accident told me that he had learned to accept his pain as part of himself. "It's me!" he explained. "Like you told us about hate," he said to me, "In my mind I try to turn the pain into love. I make it into a loyal friend who shares my life with me," he told me. "Since I adopted this attitude I think that I might actually miss the pain if it stopped hurting. I know that my attitude may not be usual but, in a way, it would be like losing a part of myself — like losing an arm or a leg. My pain puts me to sleep at night when I listen to it," and he added, "at daytime it reminds me that I'm alive!" He was pleased when I told him that I would put what he told me about how he handled his pain in the book I was writing. It gave him the hope that a reader with chronic pain might benefit from his approach.

These stories may be what seem like unusual exceptions among people who have worked out ways to handle chronic pain. Many of them used some form of transcending. It remains true that the majority of people who suffer from chronic pain frequently complain about it, either verbally or by gestures. Those to whom they complain should be aware that they are helping the victim of the pain by sympathetically listening.

In summary, people who suffer from chronic pain and who wish to use the techniques employed in transcending therapy must attempt to "jump over their pain," to reach for something that lies beyond it. This is not easy to do, especially initially. Usually the bigger picture that would make their pain more tolerable is their total life experience. Unfortunately, some cases of chronic pain contracted in the early years of life, narrow down to be their only experience. Creative evolution demands that these people find something else to live for — especially something that is creative. When some who suffered from chronic pain were asked how they felt, they answered without thinking, "Okay!" or, "good enough." The less often they think about their pain the more they can focus on other aspects of the events in their lives and the less their pain will disturb them. In short, if you suffer from chronic pain you must not allow the pain to become the main focus of your life!

MENTAL PAIN

Thus far we have discussed mainly physical pain. Now let us turn some of our attention to the mental pain we all must endure at times because we are sensitive human beings with a capacity for sympathy and sadness. It often seems that animals share the capacity for grief with human beings. However, there are few methods or doctrines, except those found in one's religious faith, that can dispel the suffering which follows the death of a loved one and causes one of our greatest sadness. The thought, if it is appropriate, "He or she will be better off," or seeing death as the end of suffering helps some people. Unless the deceased person has been suffering, death always comes as a shock. It reminds us that the length of our own life is limited. Transcending sorrow with beautiful thoughts and memories is a good way to lessen our feelings of deep sadness. Better still, and closer to transcending it, is to turn sorrow into something positive. It may be the best thing we can do when we have lost a loved one.

I found an example of what I mean in a *Reader's Digest* (February 2001). It contained a true story about a young woman named Kellie Martin, who lost her beloved sister with whom she had grown up and from whom she had never been separated. The president of the American Autoimmune Related Diseases Association wrote, "Kellie has been able to look beyond her grief (of the death of her sister), and turn it into something positive." Kellie, herself, wrote how she handled her grief. She stated, "Just as important as keeping the memory of a loved one in your mind and your heart is moving *beyond* (italics are mine) the tragedy and doing something positive in their name." The moving "beyond" is a way to transcend and overcome things that disturb us that we have advised people to do in this book. This may be a good time to think of a deceased as having made a "dent" in the world that helped to shape it to become a better place to live. This is far better than thinking that a person is simply "gone" and even more helpful than that, he or she is living in heaven collecting rewards there for having lived a good life. What "the dent" implies is that people do not live in vain if they had a kind or a constructive life or received and gave love to someone.

I offer the poem below that deals with death of a loved one. The poem is taken from my book of poems published in 1995.

Death Has Taken Someone You Love

Death has taken someone you love
Be glad that your loved one does not share your grief
For those who leave us there is only peace
You are the one deprived — not your loved one.
There is comfort in this.

Life is always the winner over death.
Death steals away life but cannot destroy it.
Every life has changed the universe by existing
Every human life adds something new to the universe
The world will never be what it was before.

Within your grief be glad
That your loved one has warmed your heart
And that this warmth is eternal
Because it has become a building block
Of all of that of which the world is made.

> Therefore think of what was,
> And not of what could have been.
> What was, existed
> What could have been did not.
> Only for the dead are these the same.
>
> Death is a reunion with the infinite
> All of us will meet it bearing gifts.
> No one leaves life empty-handed,
> The kind of life we lived is our gift to the infinite
> And, believe it or not, it says, "thanks."

This poem gives every human being something to live for. Saying "thanks" is meant to be a symbolic way of recognizing the kind of life which a loved one lived and its, perhaps silent, impact on the future of all human life. Death gives us the opportunity to turn something negative into something positive. We can learn this from flowers that wilt but bear new blossoms. The reader will find other comments about death in Chapter Eight.

What is said here about the death of a loved one applies equally to all of the major tragedies that may occur in our lives. We must look *beyond* them and, if we can, turn them into something positive. As I have said before, the desire to do so is a form of doing so. This is what we tried to do with temptation which is the subject of the next chapter. In the following chapter we suggest how we may transcend temptation. After reading the next chapter some of us will find that temptation may not be what we thought it was.

Chapter Seven

How to Transcend Temptation

Temptation is not well understood. At times it seems to play a very important role in our lives. What really is it? Had someone asked me this question before I wrote this book, I would have pictured an overweight person on a diet who experiences temptation when offered a delicious slice of cream pie. I would have thought of the pie and the person — not about the temptation.

We think of the things and people that tempt us but not of temptation as an interesting characteristic in itself. Perhaps that is because "temptation" is a scary word that usually implies that we are heading for trouble. Few of us have ever considered what is *good* about temptation. One good thing about temptation is that it is a signal of trouble ahead at a time when we still can back off and avoid it.

Temptation is all around us. Why then hasn't there been more written on the subject of temptation in the literature of behavioral science? It is seldom scientifically studied as a thing in itself. One reason for the lack of research on the subject is that "temptation" becomes no more than an unattached word when it is studied alone. One can't see it or touch it. Unfortunately, abstractions are not often grist for the mills of modern psychological research. It can loosen our thoughts from their mooring. Editors of professional journals primarily seek articles which contain many references to what other experts have already written on the subject. They are tempted to protect their selections of the subject matter that they print. As I have already said, "temptation is all around us."

In life, temptation has a paradoxical function in that it can play a major role in keeping us out of trouble. We may be surprised to learn that much good can be said about it. It is interesting and instructive to explore the theological and psychological roles of temptation in human life. When we do so, we learn a great deal about ourselves as well as about human problems. A search for the meaning of temptation gives us a glimpse into the depth of our human nature. In its simplest terms, temptation occurs when there is an opportunity to do something that is either wrong, dangerous — or, let's apply it to modern life — too expensive. Those are its negative aspects. Because temptation also tells us when to transcend, we shall see that we can circumvent temptation's negative qualities. However, to be able to do this we must view it as a warning signal — a red traffic light. We are all apt to think of traffic signals as very handy and useful. Therefore, most people normally resist the impulse to ignore them.

In the Judeo-Christian tradition, temptation plays a central role. It describes humans as destined to experience temptation but not to yield to it. The Bible relates how Adam and Eve yielded to temptation that was maliciously presented by Satan in the guise of a serpent. Adam and Eve were tempted to taste the forbidden fruit of the tree of knowledge. The Bible tells us that for their disobedience, God expelled them from paradise. However, one could put it positively, as I have already said. Experiencing temptation can actually help us to avoid trouble by alerting us in advance that we are heading into it.

People who cannot take responsibility for their own actions find it useful to blame the Devil. To do so is convenient even if it is not convincing. When I served as an expert witness in criminal trials, I recall a defendant who pleaded not guilty by claiming that the Devil had invaded his mind at the time he committed the crime. He was perfectly sincere when he insisted that he was not at fault because he was "possessed." We have read about people who were exorcised by religious rituals because they thought that the Devil had "taken possession of their soul."

No one in the past, when the belief in an actual manipulating devil was wide-spread, realized how helpful it was for humankind to blame a non-human being for things that went wrong. Now, too often, instead of a devil some member or members of our own species are dehumanized so that they may be blamed for whatever goes wrong. In neurologically sophisticated societies, a low level of the neurotransmitter, serotonin, in the cerebral cortex may be blamed instead. Others may attempt to excuse their actions by blaming their crimes on defective genes.

However, someone who is able to transcend is able to avoid using other people as scapegoats. It would be a relief for all of us if we could blame our misdeeds on something other than our fellow human beings. Instead of incessant warfare and terrorism, a Devil whom we could blame for everything that goes wrong anywhere in the world is what humankind could use right now. It might be more realistic for us to try to transcend blaming anyone and, thereby, create a more just and kinder world.

In some places we have already discovered that computers can serve as scapegoats or as alternatives to Devils. I have heard "computer error" or "the computer is down" as reasons given by banks, stores, and individuals, to explain why things weren't done right or were not ready when they had been promised. An electronic devil to blame for our mistakes would herald the electronic progress of modernity. Alternately, perhaps, we could learn to admit the mistakes we make and use them as lessons that we must learn to gain maturity as a species. The time has come to recognize temptation as, perhaps, a most reliable guide to the presence of danger. Looked at it this way, temptation may be viewed as our friend and teacher.

If we want to see it this way we can imagine that, in spirit, Lucifer still is in the picture in the modern world. He may be imagined as active as ever with his bright red lantern shedding light on the acts that lead up to doing evil. He can not free himself entirely from his past — none of us can. His red light is always visible to our mind's eye if we look around. He is the charismatic perpetrator of evil, who throughout human history has been identified as a supernatural antagonist of humankind. If we are on the watch for him we can mobilize our resolve not to become his victims. To transcend temptation by looking the other way rather than to yield to it, may save us.

Babylonian, Chaldean, Persian, Zoroastrian and Egyptian mythology portrayed evil, that is part of our disposition and our human history, in animal or semi-human forms or in a combination of the two. Eastern religions explain the existence of good and evil by viewing duality as a necessary condition of human life. The topics of this chapter are world-wide concerns of human beings since ancient times. Some people possess a nervous system that may actually seek temptations in order to experience them. The anticipation of danger helps them to maintain an interest in life. Obviously, then, imagining the Devil's warning lantern gives them no reason to pause and retreat. Those who prefer risks over safety will interpret temptation as a go-ahead signal. People having this temperament may be found in jails and hospitals. A disproportionate number of them die young. Others who were lucky, become heroes and role models for the young in our current society. This is unfortunate because the result of such false "heroism" creates the wrong kind of role models for impressionable young people who attempt to imitate them.

If we can guard against oversimplification, we can clarify concepts that have temptation at their source. These usually have an inherent vagueness built into them as, for example, "evil" has. Transcending temptation can strengthen our second human nature every time we use it. Let's look at it another way and ask, "Could the perception of goodness and evil represent an evolutionary departure from the randomness of biological evolution?" If we excluded all the supernatural aspects, goodness in human interaction might be viewed as a survival technique for things and concepts beyond the self-concern which the "survival of the fittest" represents.

Recent studies suggest that 500 million years ago the ancestors of bees, spiders, scorpions and horseshoe crabs parted evolutionary company with crustaceans and insects which had only green and ultraviolet photo receptor pigments in their visual equipment. They added blue. This additional pigment enabled them to become sensitive to a larger range of colors. It made sense to believe that by adding a color, sensitivity was an adaptation to the color of flowers from which bees obtain their nectar.

We are told that recent research at New York University suggests it was the other way around. The evolutionary innovation that increased the visual acuity of insects to colors occurred *before* there were any colored blossoms on earth. This reversed previous thinking which was based on the logical assumption that there must have been other adaptive reasons for this evolutionary innovation. Likewise, reason, for the existence of concepts such as goodness and evil may not be easily discernible by reasoning backwards. Like all things that come into being that take a certain amount of evolution to manifest, their potentiality must have been inherent in the universe from its start. This concept of reality can help us in clarifying our thinking about what is possible in the universe and for humankind.

GOODNESS AND EVIL

It has been estimated that there were 50 billion species on earth before humans arrived. The concept of goodness and evil is confined to our species by the limitations of animal imagination and perception. Our capacity to envision morality makes us different from all other creatures that exist on earth. There may, or may not be anything that resembles us elsewhere in the universe. The human imagination tends to project evil and goodness onto thousands of things and circumstances where they do not belong. We should bear in mind that "evil" cannot be found in the dictionary of natural selection. In the animal world alpha males dominate harems, fowl establish pecking orders, and social species chase intruders from their established territories. There's nothing in their make-up that cautions them not to be selfish except fear of conflict with higher ranking creatures of their kind. Some female spiders devour their smaller-sized male sexual partners. Some humans may see evil in nature after witnessing a terrified young gazelle held in the forelegs of a predator, about to tear it apart. Nature, however attaches no judgmental labels to the food chain or anything else that happens that seems cruel to us. The only considerations in nature are tied to survival, extinction, and obedience to its laws.

Modern Darwinism claims that we humans also are only motivated solely by these considerations. I have stated my argument against this view in my book *Genetic Engineering, Yes, No, or Maybe?* (2000). Humans have the "unnatural" ability to rise above the limitations of indifference to suffering. As creatures of nature we conform to it, but as humans we regret that we are compelled to do so and sometimes we don't. Signs of guilt from our participation in the food chain are as old as history itself. This is manifested in many cultures by food taboos. I will just say that some neolithic hunters conceived of their prey as offering themselves voluntarily to be eaten by humans. Certainly, this reduces the guilt associated with killing them.

Conceptions of good and evil involve more than intelligence or good judgment. It takes our unique capacity to conceive of abstractions. We can see that transcending in many ways requires us to make abstractions. Dictionaries usually define an *abstraction* as "a mental separation of a thing from its quality." One could put this as the ability to view something concretely in its physical dimensions and at the same time appreciate its utility. Abstractions are used in transcending because they enable us to respond to something that isn't always immediately apparent or available to our senses. This entails the capacity to envision the large picture view from seeing only the small picture. For example, we need witness only one good deed to recognize the existence of goodness in the world. By the use of an abstraction, a one dollar theft can be viewed as stealing in general, merely by applying to such an act the concept of dishonesty. We need only to see or hear that there is one person suffering to envision suffering anywhere in the world. Evil acts are, likewise time-spanning. To conceive or transcend the temptation of street drugs used by some students in numerous High Schools in American cities may serve as an example. It is that temptation either warns us of danger or leads us to the act.

Chapter Eight

When Will We Rise Above Ourselves?

In the twentieth century some physical anthropologists came to the conclusion that evolution had finished its job with humankind. This was because they saw no need for us to evolve further anatomical advantages.

We did not need a covering of fur in cold climates because we learned to drape ourselves in animal skins and remain warm. Nature did not have to endow us with sharp claws to help us survive because our ancestors learned how to chip sharp knives from stones and these served them better than claws. We learned how to control fire. There was no reason for us to wait for evolution to extend the reach of humans, because we could fashion spears, and make bows and arrows for hunting. Human beings' unique human brains more than compensated us for any anatomical limitations.

Those who held this view did not take into account an ongoing "creative evolution," a term used by those who believe that a different kind of evolution continues in the minds of humans when physical evolution (except for minor changes) ended. Creative evolution does not produce an extra arm or leg but rather an advanced mind-set. By means of creative evolution humans brought a new characteristic into the universe itself —

goodness for goodness's own sake — and not primarily to aid survival. Goodness did not really exist in nature because nature is neutral in all things. However, it became an aspect of a second human nature, which as we have seen, is necessary for transcending as we use the term in this book. Biological evolution permitted nothing to interfere with the spreading of genes. Creative evolution, however, made it possible for our species to forge new concepts, such as human values that exist entirely for themselves. From these, human idealism was born. We should remember that, in contrast, biological evolution is described as totally opportunistic and that all genetic changes in living creatures are thought to be caused by random variation, that is, by chance alone.

Luck is therefore seen as playing a major role in biological evolution. Luck occurs when one species develops the genes required to be able to adjust more efficiently than competing species to the demands of the natural environment — whatever it may consist of at the time. This "luck" Darwin called "natural selection" and that is a good name for what he had in mind. Neutral nature "selects" those who will live and those who will die. It does this mindlessly, but according to its laws, that create some favorable and some unfavorable conditions for certain species. Success, in an evolutionary sense, is defined as producing fertile offsprings, which, in turn, have fertile offsprings. Therefore evolutionary success of any living organism is manifested entirely by the capacity to spread genes that conform best to the needs of the environment. As previously mentioned, for many species this gives rise to one of the most cruel of all the phenomena on earth — the carnivorous food chain which is based on the command — kill to eat, or be killed and be eaten.

There are theories of evolution that emphasize the mutual dependency of some species upon other species. They live together in harmonious and symbiotic relationships. Symbiosis refers to the living together of two dissimilar organisms in a mutually beneficial relationship in their natural state. However, let us remember that only by chance does it work out that way. All symbiotic relationships might just as well have developed to be more like their opposites, such as, for example, a fungus species, genus *Cardyceps,* which fatally invades the bodies of ants and other insects. The fungus then grows antler-like structures from within the corpse which will then shoot up spores to be dispersed by the breeze. Usually dead ants fall to the forest floor, but fungus-infected ants clamp down on a leaf as they die. This places the fungus where it can reach other tree-dwelling victims. There are a number of similar gruesome scenarios like this in nature. The challenge for humans is not to imitate these scenarios either actually or symbolically. Unfortunately, with our first human nature we have chosen to imitate nature in many ways throughout our history. Our second human nature has clashes with Darwin's view of evolution and with the biologists who recommend how classical evolution is best applied to humankind. Hence some humanists have developed the idea of creative evolution as more suitable for humanity.

In its forward march, Darwin's view of evolution creates victims especially between phases, stages, and levels of development. The easy availability of firearms and deadly weapons creates opportunities for antisocial individuals and some mentally deranged ones, to commit crimes and increase destruction throughout the world. In the long run, destructive power in the hands of some people will require them to hold back their anger and act with responsibility toward each other or perish. A human nature which I have referred to as the second human nature, could not have come into being had not a first human nature preceded it.

It is remarkable that we are almost totally unaware of our second human nature's role in human life. It is our second human nature from which goodness and idealism are derived. We may find an inexact shadow of it in Sigmund Freud's sex-dominated system of psychology; specifically, in what used to be called the "superego." But as I have already stated in previous chapters, it was incomplete because it was thought to have come into existence solely through environmental exposures. Now we know that our second human nature came into existence from hereditary characteristics that made it, to some extent, both a product of genetics and new ways of thinking that led us to goodness.

In mythology and religions there is the recognition of human goodness often projected onto gods and angels. In science we can only see technological change occurring in an age of ever more efficient computers, advances in quantum physics, and in molecular biology. We fail to see that at some time in the past, creative evolution accompanied Homo sapiens sapiens' biological evolution. Without it there could be no transcending such as we have described in this book.

Our second human nature is presently only very poorly understood. Its components may include the human power of abstraction, the long period of human infancy, our human ability to formulate language, human intelligence, and a mixed-up human quality which we still can't quite understand, which we call, "spirituality." It is a greater wonder that we fail to fully realize that our fantastic human imagination can break every law in the universe in imagination. True, it's only in imagination, but what other creature can do this? It may take us much time in the future to grasp the full significance of this.

However, the ancient writers of the Hebrew Bible must have had an inkling of what was happening in human creative evolution since they placed our role in the universe as "a little lower than the angels" whereas at the present time our scientists see us as merely a little higher than the animals. Actually it isn't a matter of "higher" or "lower" but of significant differences in the look-alike and act-alike evolutionary biological developments of living creatures. Molecular biologists have discovered that we have only about 30,000 genes when previous to mapping the human genome it was estimated that humans had over a 100,000. But this does not reveal the true story about ourselves. We have almost the identical genes as the chimpanzees. We are using human genes inserted into pigs to create human medications. However, we are not chimpanzees and we are not pigs. But we are finding out by research in genetic engineering that our differences from animals are complex and not a matter of genes alone.

Part of our problem is that human beings are very impatient to grow up into angels whereas in terms of our species' age in evolution, we are merely very gifted young children and we act like children would be expected to act. The invention of our human kind of goodness from which no reward other than the existence of goodness is gained, started us in a new direction that has gone far beyond natural selection. We don't know what other forms of life inhabit the universe but as far as we can tell, human morality introduces new elements into the universe itself as did the preceding organic evolution. It forces us to think deeply about what occurred to the nascent universe besides its Big Bang. We are told that the Big Bang occurred an estimated 12 billion years or so, ago.

"Big Bang" is the colloquial way of referring to the beginning of our universe. It is worth thinking about the fact that everything that has occurred thus far or will ever occur in the future in the universe originally had to exist in potentiality at the start of, or before the "bang." By definition, nothing can happen without having a *potentiality* for it to occur. This fact leads us humbly to acknowledge how little we really know — even if we should be "only a little lower than the angels." For example, we do not yet find the creative evolution represented by human goodness listed among scientific breakthroughs.

In preferring goodness over evil, nature lent us a hand. Natural selection provided people who were good with a greater opportunity for survival. The idea is simple. If I scratch your back when you want me to, you are likely to scratch mine when I want you to, and we'll both be better off. These are the reciprocal aspects of goodness acknowledged by evolutionists but that is as far as they go. Goodness has survival value for ourselves and our species which evil does not have. Our purely biological motivation for goodness may have given us a running start which headed us into the right direction. It was followed by a quantum leap into a new direction which could only be achieved by a species that had the kind of imagination combined with the technical know-how required to send one of its kind to the moon. It also needed and possessed the spirituality it took to build pyramids and cathedrals.

I have previously mentioned that with our human imagination we can break every law in the universe. For example we can go much faster than the speed of light in our imagination. No living thing besides humans could ever do that. To those who would say deprecatingly, "but only in imagination," I would like to remind them once again that Einstein said wisely that imagination is more important than knowledge. All great human achievements first originated in the human imagination. Unfortunately, our imagination also has a very negative side to it that has done a lot of damage to the world. I feel compelled to mention this and will do so in the next chapter.

The German philosopher Immanuel Kant's definition of human goodness may also have helped us in this effort by highlighting the uniqueness of goodness in nature. It changes the struggle to spread genes into the struggle to spread ideas. For many humans, idea-survival has become a symbolic substitute for gene-survival. Idea-survival consists to a large extent of conflicting concepts on "what is the best way to be good?" In spite of the powerful commercial interests that underlie many wars, no one would be willing to risk their lives in any war unless the forward echelons in the battle carried the banner of goodness. Only for this reason are the words to the hymn compelling: "Onward Christian soldiers, marching as to war"— a war meant for establishing goodness in the world! All wars are "sold" to its participants under the advertised name of "goodness" even if in their actions, exactly the opposite occurs.

Let us think this over. According to current biological thinking nature endows all forms of life with the single-minded goal to succeed in gene-spreading. This is the overriding reason science offers for the present existence of living things as they are. Yet scientific research has found such exceptions as the peacock's long beautiful feathers, which are a hindrance to flight and survival, but are an asset to courtship. Scarcely explained by Darwinian theory are facts exemplified by some species of female cockroaches who prefer to copulate with males that have odors attractive to them but who are not necessarily the most fit to perpetuate the species. Some species, even if they are far lower on the hierarchy of living things have demonstrated the ability to select what they actually prefer instead of what is best for their survival. Yet they are still able to survive because they have other strengths.

This may be a revolution of a quality that exists merely to exist seen at all levels of life. Among humans the implication of this revolution may be represented in the transition from "me" to "other than me" and this is not yet grasped by the majority of people. Even some leading scientists remain fixated on the struggle for existence by natural selection alone instead of the new struggle for the existence of ideas by human selection which may, over time, replace the former. Our unique transition from gene-spread, directed by our first human nature, to idea-spread, orchestrated by our second human nature, enters the picture when we think of creative evolution.

The Mystery of Human Goodness and Morality

We must consider the question raised by two psychologists, C. Daniel Batson and Elizabeth R. Thompson, at the University of Kansas when they asked the question, "Why Don't Moral People Act Morally?" After researching the question they concluded that "Failure of moral people to act morally is usually attributed to either learning deficits or situational pressures." In addition, the authors found that many would-be moral people abandon their intentions during periods of lack of motivation, and when the cost of integrity becomes overwhelming. As a part of their conclusions the authors note, "There are persistent and perplexing questions still to be answered." The reader at this point discovered that lack of motivation may be due to a failure of a person's second human nature. The cause of the failure is often explained as due to a person's hypocrisy. If so how would we interpret such hypocrisy? We should think of it the way the 17th Century French epigrammatist, Francois La Rochefoucauld did when he wrote: "Hypocrisy is homage vice pays to virtue." In other words, virtue, goodness, and morality are respected by the hypocrites, as they are by all people, or there would not be any hypocrisy.

One objective of this chapter is to point out to the reader that on the average, humans perceive goodness as a great treasure in spite of all the selfish impulses stemming from their first human nature. Our major human task at this juncture of our human history is to make goodness as we have defined it — ethics, morality, compassion, and world togetherness — exciting and inspiring. To do this we must make goodness become more than just a duty or something to be done in order to avoid divine, parental, or societal punishment. Another problem consists of the interpretation of goodness. Various world religions have tried to define "goodness" for millennia. They have had a measure of success but they must go beyond religious dogmas, which compete with each other and tie goodness into holiness alone, instead of including it also as an aspect of behavioral science.

In my clinical practice I have interviewed teen-age youths who were ashamed to be considered as being good. Peer pressure forces some youngsters to assume an external image of "toughness" and heartlessness. Rebelliousness is characteristic of youths in many cultures. Thereby, the young undergo a period of learning. I have found in my assessment of young delinquents that a considerable number of their antisocial acts stem from their feelings of worthlessness and a lack of opportunity for them to play a useful role in society — in other words, they think that they lack the opportunity to be "good." Many of the antisocial feelings seen in juvenile gangs world-wide, stem from this self-imposed exclusion.

Many antisocial teenagers are law-abiding after they mature and become gainfully employed. Their employment provides them with the chance to contribute to human needs through their work which unconsciously, if not consciously, is equated with goodness. We may be unaware that this occurs even among the most materialistic of us who often verbalize earning money as the sole objective of employment. Deep within themselves even most of the money-driven people who earn their wealth honestly feel that through their work they are making a contribution to the world. The deprivation of a chance to contribute to human goodness through work is the most destructive element of all. Even those who work in a munitions factory that produce bombs feel compelled to view themselves as working for human good. I have made it a point to interview some of them from time to time and consistently have obtained answers that indicate that they feel good about their work.

It explains why some people with excellent retirement pensions find retirement almost unbearable. Significantly, they never seem to have understood that it is neither their spare energy nor boredom that causes their restive problems. It is, instead, their inability to continue to do something for others that really bothers them most. Many leave their homes and search for entertainment of any type in order to divert their thought from their real preferences of doing some good in the world. Often they have to struggle also in deciding whether to use their first human nature or their second one. Also, unrecognized by most people is that our fear of death to a large degree consists of facing an eternity without being able to do anything to assist others. On an unconscious level the lack of opportunity to do good is what bothers many people the most about the thought of death. This desire, unrealistic as it may often be, explains why some people cling desperately to life.

It appears as if I have mentally resuscitated Jean Jacques Rousseau, (1712- 1778) the French philosopher and political theorist of the period of the Enlightenment. He held that humans were basically good in their natural state but were corrupted by civilization. Rousseau profoundly influenced the literature and philosophy in the 19th century but was discredited later by explorations that provided additional information about primitive peoples. He erred in that he saw goodness only among people he designated, "in their natural state uncontaminated by civilization." However, the will to goodness can be discerned in all populations provided their motives are fully understood and correctly interpreted.

Yesterday's truths are often today's misconceptions. We have heard many times that goodness is largely culture determined. However, recent scientific research suggests that today we must add to this that the limits of cultures are, at least partially, genetically determined. If there is a common thread that runs through various cultures it is the consideration for others. We may think that this applies only to our own people, nation, or tribe. However, hopefully with time, it will be recognized that it encompasses all human beings. The seeds are there even if not yet flowering. A Good Samaritan story wins universal human approval. Goodness needs time and opportunity to grow. And goodness for its own sake (instead as a subterfuge for causing the spread of genes) is a new child in our universe. It needs time and opportunity to grow.

In the past the most heinous and virulent conflicts among humans arose from different views of what constitutes goodness in the eyes of the combatants. Although it may be perceived totally differently, it is the universal calling card for each warring side. Goodness for humanity has always been the banner under which actions take place in marketing new ideas on how we should live — be they socialism, communism, capitalism, dictatorship, tribalism, as well as in embracing conflicting religious ideas. It is only the design of the banner that differs, never the claim of supporting goodness.

Bishop Tutu of South Africa said of humans, "We all hunger for goodness." Yes, a hungry person does not possess peace of mind. It is every human being's obligation to do what ever he or she can to make certain that we do not wipe out the human species by the starvation of goodness. If we are positioned to participate in this effort, we ourselves will gain peace of mind because we have improved the opportunity for goodness to exist in our world. There is nothing that can bring us greater satisfaction than this because this is how we rise above ourselves.

Chapter Nine

Creative Evolution is the Key to Transcending

Henri Bergson, (1859-1941) the French sociologist and Nobel laureate accounted for the existence of human goodness by visualizing it as the product of creative evolution. Creative evolution is a human-created evolution. It includes a people's history, traditions, and values. These differ over time and among various cultural and geographical groups. The differences can create the illusion that members of other groups belong to different species. Thus it divides the human species, with its single genome, into segments each of which vie for the title — "human being." Due to our superior human imagination, an ancient and, in some ways self-rewarding human game, generally called, "prejudice," accompanies it.

In his theory of creative evolution, Bergson did not deny our animal origins, nor that animals share many of our human emotions. Beyond these, mutations must have occurred when Homo sapiens sapiens evolved leading to greatly increased intelligence, imagination, and an ability for abstractions that provided us with a capacity for idealism. Our human idealism from which our capacity to transcend is derived, is humankind's secret adventure and I hope to show that it is of great significance. It helps to distinguish transcending from other kinds of mental "jumping overs" that have an entirely different objective such as blocking, denying, or substituting. All of these also share certain characteristics with transcending but are derived from our first human nature of "self first," devoid of idealism.

The English biologist, Thomas Henry Huxley (1825-1895) maintained that a human being is "not degraded because he shares many instincts with lower animals." He is raised up because he has developed some of those instincts and controlled others to create our second human nature as I describe it in this book. But he did not deny that goodness and all that it entails may have had animal origins. In some ways its origins may be explained by a series of mutations which occurred in the creation of Homo sapiens sapiens.

Huxley wrote:

> In comparing civilized man with the animal world, one is as the Alpine traveler, who sees the mountains soaring into the sky ... he can hardly discern where the roseate peaks end and where the clouds of heaven begin. Surely the awestruck voyager may be excused if, at first, he refuses to believe ... that these glorious masses are, after all, the hardened mud of primal seas or the cooled slag of subterranean furnaces ... raised by inward forces to that place of proud and seemingly inaccessible glory.

I shall use Huxley's poetic statements above, in an analogy. The "mud" and the "slag" represent goodness that exists merely as a means to an end. The genuine goodness for which humans hunger is represented by "the roseate peaks ... where the clouds of heaven begin." Thus goodness was seeded and took root among one of the youngest of species on earth — the human species. There, it resides as an infant and relies on us, who are not much older in the time clock of life, to create the environment required for its survival. Thus it causes problems for us.

We need additional centuries to provide for its full maintenance. This gives every human being a measure of responsibility for helping nature move into a new direction beyond physical survival that may occasionally bypass our first human nature. We must transmit this message to the young people in our world today. The analogy we may use is that the essence of our second human nature is like the "glorious mountains raised by inward forces of nature" which give human life a special meaning and significance.

Goodness falls into a new class of things valued entirely for themselves with no other uses than that humans want to live in a world where it exists. To argue that goodness has an ulterior motive in that it satisfies a human desire is meaningless tautology in that it merely says that humans desire a goodness without an ulterior motive. The beauty of flowers, and beauty in general, approaches this idea but differs in that no inner struggle is required in the wish for beauty. Goodness often requires some measure of struggle with the lower brain centers that remain fixated on self-centered gratification.

Nor is human goodness merely the product of domestication. Certainly domesticated animals also behave as if they were good. The human goodness that is unique in nature is partially genetically rooted. This does not mean that humans carry a gene for goodness. Instead, it indicates that the genetically-based groundwork for goodness is in place in the human genome. The long period of infant helplessness after birth contributes a biological need for caring for the young far beyond that of any other species. The combination of genes that have a behavioral expression consists of human imagination, capacity for high level abstractions, the long period of infant helplessness, a thirst for novelty, and other things (perhaps not all of them known at this time), which contribute to the invention of the human kind of goodness. Those who realize that the environment sometimes serves as a trigger for the expression of certain genetic tendencies will have no difficulty in understanding this.

Therefore human goodness stems from the combination of human genes that allows for a new kind of goodness within an environment that nourishes self-other identification. The result is a breakthrough in nature and a first step in revealing a new dimension in evolution which hitherto had hit its ceiling in intelligence. We should be aware of the fact that the potentiality for the human kind of goodness must have been in place when the present universe began. I have pointed out before that the possibility of anything to exist occurred before it could exist. Seen this way credit must be given for the potentiality of things. The recognition of this has led many of the world's people to a belief in a God who is seen as the embodiment of goodness. It was not always so. The gods of earlier people were not always very nice. They were vengeful, resentful, capricious, and sometimes downright mean. The evolution of goodness parallels the human perception of God seen as good rather than purely punitive.

By probing the neural processing of written words, researchers have found that the brain must perpetually activate neural systems designed by evolution for entirely dissimilar tasks. By using PET brain scans, neuroscientists have also discovered that the brain uses different neural circuits for reading silently and reading aloud. Still additional areas of the brain are used for comprehending what has been read. Jack M. Fletcher at the University of Texas at Houston points out that "Speech is a biologically evolved skill." Anthropologists tell us that we have had speech for as long as 4 million years. We have had written language for 4,000 years. We are biologically destined to speak, but not to read or write. Nevertheless, we humans do read and write regardless of our "biological destiny," and so it is with goodness. The pursuit of goodness has changed our destiny and given a purpose to our life. It is to make the world safe enough to allow goodness to exist.

Our evaluation of humankind as bad when we listen to the media is incomplete and superficial. We have been unaware that our unflattering view of humankind is in itself an unmistakable sign of our human goodness. Only "a hunger for goodness" as Bishop Tutu put it, could produce condemnation of a world in which insufficient goodness exists. We do not look deeply enough to find this hunger. We do not look for it in the common man and woman in the long stretch of human history. We fail to see it in the ancient legends. For example, a legend about Genghis Khan, the ruthless 13th Century conqueror, describes him as telling his victims, "if you had not committed great sins God would not have sent a punishment like me upon you." In an argument on whether Genghis Khan actually said this, the main point is lost. The main point is that the legend perpetuated by his loyal Mongolian followers implies that this fierce and merciless killer was portrayed as an instrument of God and therefore served the cause of goodness.

Some things are not capable of existing in our universe. Perpetual motion is said to be one of these. The laws of nature cannot be circumvented. Many creative people assume that they have produced something totally new and original. We tend to forget the fact that the *possibility* for existence must precede existence. The recognition of this truism has led many people in the world to a belief in a God who is described by most religions as the embodiment of possibility.

Ironically, prejudice and hate are made of almost the same ingredients as goodness, just as -1 and +1 have something in common. Yet they pull gravitation into opposite directions. It is difficult to see that love and hate are shipmates who sail the seas on the same boat. We have split them into two human categories for our convenience and thus they must stay. Love is the product of the second human nature whereas hate stems from emotion filtered through the first human nature. What causes this division of emotions? One of several possible answers is *dehumanization.*

The first human nature adds a measure of dehumanization to the mix and dehumanization is a minus sign. Only a minority of neurologists would explain the minus sign as an absence of specific brain cells required for humans to identify with each other and develop empathy. More of them refuse to give the -1: a purely physiological basis. Much more research is required on this subject. However, one fact is clear, our superb human imagination can make other members of our species appear less than human. We even give our enemies special names as our soldiers do in warfare. Then we can hate and kill without guilt because in our minds we are not killing human beings. Therefore we commit no atrocities. We humans have perpetrated and some of us still do, the most heinous crimes upon our fellow humans by not viewing them as fellow human beings.

Unhindered by complexity, an individual can focus his longing for idealism on a single ethnicity, tribe, race, nationality or religion, and dehumanize all others. Dehumanizing members of our species is easy and can efficiently be done with our agile human power of imaginative circumvention. Dehumanizing invariably accompanies murder and destruction of property. It is the essential tool of terrorists. Those who hurt dehumanized human beings are, in their minds as well as by their own definition, *not* hurting human beings.

Throughout our history this has been used to divide our species into "good guys" and "bad guys." The imaginary "bad guys" usually are members of helpless minorities who can be treated with horrible cruelty by the self-appointed "good guys." They use them as scapegoats, hate them, dehumanize them, and, at times, torture them and kill them regardless of whether they are innocent men, women, or children. Furthermore, the perpetrators feel good and righteous about doing it. Later, during humankind's more enlightened moments, these perpetrators may be called "inhuman," "barbarous," or "sociopaths." However, I feel that none of us can escape with a clear conscience, from this not uncommon abnormality of our first human nature, when it combines with our human imagination to commit humankind's most evil acts. Then we must all suffer with shame that our species has the capability to fall into such massive paranoia which our unique imagination supports.

An example follows. A recent Los Angeles newspaper headline read, "Teens Who Hate." The article quoted a teen-age racist's explanation of his hate for other than "whites." He said, "We are just waking up our Aryan brothers and taking care of ourselves. We get lots of little kids with us. I feel like they're all my kids."

Had he applied his warm feelings to *all* of the "kids" that comprise our species, he would have been considered to be a good person and admired as an idealist. Prompted by his normal hunger for goodness and propelled by his impatience, his ignorance, and a personal sense of failure, he took the shortcut of dehumanizing a portion of our species. Thereafter, he became a dangerous racist. Dehumanizing is a steep price to pay for satisfying a hunger for idealism. Humans can not ignore this hunger without depriving themselves of the capacity to transcend. It is not surprising that an increasing number of people turn to bizarre cults, in their search for a short-cut for sharing in the goodness for which, as I have said before, Bishop Tutu of South Africa, correctly said, "the world hungers." All the time, idealism exists in reverse and its backward movement appears in the first human nature while its forward movement is lodged in the second human nature. There it remains for us to experience, but only if we open our eyes to it. Only if we transcend the evil in the world will we, in time, have peace on earth which must be preceded by peace in the human mind. Those who can agree with this will find that their personal transcending becomes much easier.

A recent study of the honesty of Americans involved a questionnaire in which persons were asked, "If you found a wallet containing a hundred dollars would you return it if you could locate the owner?" A large majority said that they would. The study was rightly faulted since there was no follow-up to find out if those who answered the questionnaire were merely trying to put themselves into a good light. The conclusion was that the study was worthless. However, an important point was missed. It was that people feel the need to portray themselves as good. Bishop Tutu and I would agree that there can only be one explanation for this need. It is a powerful hunger for goodness among human beings.

The hard road to goodness which requires sacrifice is still out of the reach of some people. This compels them to take shortcuts. Dehumanizing others is a frequent shortcut. With the help of their marvelous imagination they can pretend that some people they dislike are not humans. Thus, unhindered by complexity, an individual can focus his longing for goodness on only a narrow segment of humankind such as on a single ethnicity, tribe, race, nationality, or religion and dehumanize all others. Dehumanizing members of our species is easy and can efficiently be done with our agile human power of imagination and our ego-defenses using circumvention. I have already mentioned that dehumanizing frequently accompanies murder and destruction of property. It is the essential tool of terrorists. It is important to remember that those who hurt dehumanized beings are, by their own definition, *not* hurting human beings.

We have come this far. Now let us examine where goodness that exists in the world today is hiding. It would be clearly visible to us if we opened our eyes to see it. We take for granted the many small acts of courtesy and kindness that occur every day all over the world. We tend not to take any consideration of things that we are accustomed to. I refer to our conventional kindness when we greet each other with "How are you?" "Good Day," "Glad to see you." Although these are usually stereotyped forms of goodness they reflect an underlying kindness. We demonstrate goodness when we give directions to people who have lost their way, hold the door open for someone to enter when we leave a building, and pick up what someone in a wheelchair has dropped to the floor. We think nothing of these acts because they are trivial. However, they would be viewed as monumental errors in a world of badness.

Sometimes it takes a natural disaster to give human goodness visibility. Many countries provide government disaster relief augmented by personal donations for victims of floods, fires, earthquakes, and other destructive natural events. At those times, we hear of people who take risks to assist victims and think of their life-saving acts as a matter of course. There is an unwritten code of fair behavior that people adhere to in nations that are free. An example is people lining up in an orderly fashion and taking their turn based on the time of their arrival when waiting at a street corner for transportation or some other services. Most people do so because they want to be fair and not solely to prevent disorder and strife. In a world of badness, the physically strongest would push aside the weaker ones and muscle their way up to the front. Among us there are vegetarians who object to nature's cruel food-chain. Some refrain from eating meat solely because of their *ethical* convictions against the idea of "eat or be eaten." How many vegetarians there are, or whether or not we agree with them, is not the point. Rather, it is that members of our species are capable of foregoing eating certain foods because it offends their concept of goodness.

What I have said about human goodness has been said before but it has received scant attention. In his book on Rudyard Kipling, Paul Mason quoted Steven Marcus. Mason wrote:

> We come to ... the secret which Kipling, like all distinguished writers have grasped about boyhood. It is that boys live a life which is passionately moral. Half of the intensity, difficulty and refractoriness of boys may be traced to the fact that their passionate moral demands on life seem in the sad course of things bound to be frustrated and betrayed....

Upon reading this we are apt to believe that what Marcus wrote does not apply to our present generation of young people. However, those who think that our civilization is mired in crime should remember that statistics show that only about 4% of the population commit more than 80% of all major crimes. This fact is obscured by the fact that 3.9 million men and women are on probation or parole in the U.S.A. with an approximate increase of 2.9 % yearly. A large number of the 4% who commit violent crimes suffer from early environmental deprivation or brain abnormality from birth. The multiplicity of factors that lead to antisocial behavior includes one theory that suggests such behavior had evolutionary advantage for children who lived in the early stone age societies. In modern times, a study revealed that an expectant mother's nutritional habits, use of drugs and alcohol, and exposure to environmental toxins may predispose the fetal brain to hyper-vigilance or aggression. We must add to these the lack of exposure to creative evolution in our homes and schools and churches.

There is a minority of other people who seem to lack any sense of morality and who do not suffer from these disabilities. Some of their behavior may stem from defective genes or brain damage of some type. Weak-minded people with poor self-images feel an impulse to imitate violent crimes that create headlines and receive much television coverage. An interesting recent finding was that teenagers with inflated self-images were often found among violent youths. However, if one penetrates deeply enough into the causes of some of these crimes one finds that many of them are committed by people who have a deep-seated dissatisfaction with themselves and humankind. In their lives they are blocked from expressing their hunger for goodness. This leads them to disguise this hunger by opting for the opposite type of behavior. As a result many search for escape routes from life by means of crimes, street drugs, alcoholism, nicotine addiction, or psychosomatic illnesses, and, an increasing number through terrorism.

In order to improve society and reduce crime we should know that many of such tragic escape attempts are rooted in a frustrated and unsatisfied hunger for goodness that seems out of reach to many young people. For a sizeable number of former wrong-doers, lasting reform followed by the realization that doing something worthwhile (something good) with their lives is not out of their reach. Transcending helped some of them discover their second human nature and that, in turn, helps them to be what has been called, "reborn" with different goals in life.

It is not surprising that the role of goodness in human life is reflected in theological literature. Heaven is reserved for good people. Hinduism maintains that only those who have lived good lives on earth can free themselves from endless births and rebirths to reach Nirvana. Taoism teaches that only those who live good lives will sleep well when their day is over. Religions tie goodness intimately to human life. Various religions have another important element in common. According to them, people who practice goodness only for the advantages it may give them — the so-called, pragmatists' goodness — will be denied rewards. It is only those who seek goodness for itself who find peace as they gain the knowledge that their lives are on the right trail to lastingly improve human society.

Let us consider some specifics. Our yearly donations to various charities in the United States can be counted in many billions. The number of volunteers in our country who work at hospitals, libraries, schools, the Peace Corps, Salvation Army, the Red Cross and so on make up a veritable army of goodness. Safe driving doesn't make headlines whereas fatal accidents do. Goodness may bore us. A bank robbery is brought to our attention while hundreds of peaceful depositors are taken for granted. Swindle, graft and corruption are topics of conversation whereas honesty seldom is. When Menninger made his observation on human badness he failed to place people's goodness on the other tray of the moral scale. Had he done so, he would have found that the sum of our invisible goodness in everyday life would overwhelmingly outweigh our visible badness.

What is bad? It is bad to gain satisfaction from hurting other people, or from indifference to their suffering, or worse to take advantage of their plight. What is good? Impulses, desires, intentions to assist other people are good. Bad and good in this sense are not opposites as they seem to be. They are worlds apart. Badness is comparable to entropy which by definition of the nature of the universe creates ever greater disorder. Goodness represents the creative forces in the universe—its overarching beauty that inspires wonder and awe.

I refer again to the recent study of the honesty of Americans which involved a questionnaire in which persons were asked, "If you found a wallet containing a hundred dollars would you return it if you could locate the owner?" It is typical of our way of thinking that the important point of the outcome of the study was missed. It was that people feel *the need* to portray themselves as good. This need reveals that the seeds of goodness are present in our species but most of us know that they have as yet, not flowered. An innovation of such magnitude in nature as idealism takes time to take hold. It is accompanied by the fact that a majority of humans refuse to live all of their lives within their first human nature and to be guided, at least some of the time, by the forward-looking values of their second human nature.

I shall summarize as follows. Among our early hominid ancestors, mutual help within a species consistent with an embryonic Golden Rule may have served only for species survival. We see this now in animals and insects. Among humans alone, this mutual help developed into a form of goodness valued for its own sake. This is a biological breakthrough which is difficult to comprehend because it is still in the making. In the 3 1/2 billion years of the evolution of life nothing comparable has happened. Among today's humans, the pursuit of goodness, traces of which exist even in our badness, replaces spreading our genes as a primary human directional thrust. How did this happen?

Goodness "graduated" from species survival as its sole *raison d'etre* to an existence for its own sake. Throughout this book I have supported my contention that the potentiality for goodness was always present as was the potentiality for birds to fly while they were still lizards and long before they evolved into birds. *The nature of the universe is such that it pushes its potentialities into existence whenever circumstances allow it to do so.*

It is not chance alone but a chance to push potentiality into reality with which we are dealing when we look at evolution. This has been generally misunderstood. We scientists have been vague about it because some things may be dangerous for scientists to say. The universe is dynamic and owes its existence to its dynamism. Its push constitutes the engine of evolution of both life and non-life. It is this dynamism that gave birth to the universe — probably the daughter of a pre-universe — and made possible a new kind of goodness hitherto unknown in nature on earth. The human brain provided the ingredients necessary for the universe to be able to actualize goodness as one of its remote potentialities. This is how science relates to religion.

Both, in their own way, assess the pre-universe and the dynamism that was required to account for it. The human achievement of the goodness to which I refer shows Darwinian evolution to be incomplete and, therefore, causes the theory of evolution as we know it now, to be misleading.

I believe that before the end of the third millennium it will be recognized as such. Over the coming centuries, the paradigm presented by the Darwinian and neo-Darwinist views of nature as they are now popularized, will do humankind a disservice. They fail to recognize Homo sapiens sapiens' greatest innovations — the unique human kind of goodness that we evolved solely because we want to use it to be the compass to guide us along the paths of our lives. Evolution accounts for its results by random selection but ignores the "push" that must accompany all random selection in order to enable anything to happen. The best example of what I mean is the embryonic flowering of the human type of goodness created by human selection instead of Darwin's random natural selection.

Human existence has changed the world. It has unveiled our second human nature which has enabled us to transcend our first. It caused people to feel *the need* to portray themselves as good. This need reveals that the seeds of goodness today are present in our species but most of us know that they have not, as yet, flowered. An innovation of such magnitude in nature as idealism requires time to take hold, to recognize, and to celebrate. In many religions we do this in the form of celebrating the birth of a great religious leader. On a personal level, we try, at times, to transcend our first human nature and sometimes, search for guidance (unfortunately, often in theory only) from the forward-looking values of our second human nature. For this to be successful, we require more experience in transcending instead of learning about psychotherapy alone. Transcending based on idealism is genuine and lasting. This distinguishes it from activities that may resemble transcending in some ways, but lack its idealism and do not achieve its results.

Chapter Ten

Transcending or Psychotherapy: What is the Difference?

Psychotherapy and transcending help to improve the quality of human life. However, their methods and goals differ. One cannot achieve the ability to transcend using the same techniques that are successful in psychotherapy. All formal psychotherapies use techniques that are designed to help people achieve adaptive, mature, and realistic attitudes towards life.

People who seek psychotherapy and those who wish to transcend face in two different directions. Psychotherapy leads persons' attention to themselves; transcending, to *beyond* themselves. Improvement in the lives of others can and does often happen when a person obtains psychotherapy. However, this would be coincidental and is not the primary purpose of psychotherapy. On the other hand, people are able to transcend even if they leave their own and the psychological shortcomings of others out of their consideration. His or her self-image does not need to concern anyone who transcends. Yet both psychotherapy and transcending tend to improve mental health but they do it in different ways. One purpose of this book is to clarify the different goals of these two approaches to mental health.

Before the advent of psychiatry people thought that demonical possession or supernatural punishment caused mental illness.

Later, in the 18th and 19th century, a lack of moral comprehension was seen as the root of mental illness. In time, this led to a more humane treatment of the mentally ill. Psychiatry began when reformers described mental aberration as a disease. The conditions I refer to here are the psychoses — mental illnesses — which differ fundamentally from emotional maladjustments (at one time called "neuroses") that may be found to some degree in almost all of us.

When I use the term, "psychotherapy" here I refer only to methods used to help those people who have emotional problems severe enough to limit their efficiency or enjoyment of life. Emotional support, which serves as psychotherapy, without the use of the term, goes on all the time between people when two or more persons give each other acceptance and approval. This can happen anywhere in ordinary situations such as at home, at work, at church, and during recreational activities. Some psychologists consider that the ability to learn, relax, rethink, or eliminate destructive habits, is the key to success in psychotherapy. These goals may be achieved in a variety of ways that do not all depend on psychotherapy.

In the early part of the 20th century, psychoanalytic therapies dominated the field of mental health. They centered on the discovery of unconscious motives and the release of repressed feelings. It was believed that self-rejection and the attempt to avoid emotional pain often led to the use of maladaptive defenses and compensations. The goal was, therefore, to gain insight into these causes and achieve self-understanding. At first, classical psychoanalysis was in full swing in its attempt to accomplish this. Later a number of modifications of classical psychoanalysis followed on the therapeutic scene. These gave the concept of maladjusted behavior a different emphasis. With the passing years, new approaches to mental health continue to be formulated. Group therapy gives each member of a group the opportunity to share experiences, and feelings, and to receive help in learning how to handle their own problems by sharing them with others in the group. Participation creates a sense of community. Behavioral therapies represent a more physiologically oriented approach to achieve mental health.

Pleasant and unpleasant responses to maladaptive behaviors (positive and negative reinforcers) can help a person relinquish maladaptive behavior. Later, cognitive therapies were introduced that encouraged a person to think positively about life. How people interpret life experiences was considered the crucial factor in adjustment. Cognitive therapy taught clients to let reasonable expectations replace the false notions of the options in life. When cognitive therapy was combined with behavioral conditioning (or "behavioral analysis" as it is now called) it joined the concept of habit relearning with cognitive principles. Other therapies that are used include imagery, meditation, release therapy, psychodrama, and one called, "paradoxical therapy," in which a stubborn patient can, at times, be stirred into opposing the therapist's orders to continue his or her maladaptive behavior.

In the mid to later part of the 20th century, transcendental meditation and other Eastern forms of therapy gained adherents in the United States. Most of these demand concentration in clearing the mind of all thoughts and concerns until a trance-like state is achieved. The term, "transcendental," should not be confused with transcending, as I use this word in the book. The two differ both in underlying philosophy and techniques.

Some therapists view their therapy as eclectic and concerned with the whole person rather than just one aspect of the person. This attitude is thought to foster a trusting client-therapist relationship. It reassures clients that they have another person involved in their problems which they are unable to solve by themselves. At the end, however, therapists avoid leaving their clients dependent on them and feel successful if their clients have gained sufficient self-assurance and maturity to solve their own problems. Psychotherapy offers clients assurances that they are not isolated and alone. That is why the success of psychotherapy often hinges on the therapist's ability to establish rapport and empathy. In some cases the ability to transcend can be facilitated if it is preceded by psychotherapy.

It is of interest that, in view of the above, a philosophy of existence — existentialism — which claims that a person's aloneness is inevitable, developed into an influential adjunct to psychotherapy. We must take a close look at existentialism, cognitive therapy, and a psychoanalytic ego defense called *sublimation* since these can appear to have misleading similarities to transcending which require clarification. First let us look a bit deeper into existentialism.

Although the movement had a number of predecessors, the beginning of existentialism is associated with the writing of Soren Kierkegaard (1813-1855), Danish philosopher and theologian, who maintained that at the highest levels a human being must have an awareness of his individuality. He felt that an awareness of one's uniqueness was necessary in order to be true to oneself. He countered Plato's perception of universal ethics. Instead, he felt that one must look within oneself to formulate them. He went further to declare that one must be totally committed to being true to one's own feelings in order to be genuinely religious. He introduced the idea of anguish at the recognition of one's helplessness and that in the process of being oneself, one is inevitably alone.

Jean Paul Sartre (1905-1980) is the name of the French writer who used the term, existentialism, to describe his own atheistic and generally pessimistic philosophy of human existence. He became internationally influential after World War II for his ideas that humans are responsible but lonely beings, adrift in a meaningless world. The need to make choices in such a world calls for personal responsibility for the consequences of the choices made. Common themes in existentialism are stress on each person's responsibility to find personal meaning in life in contrast to prescribed universal meaning, individual freedom of choice and the responsibility that choosing entails. These ideas eventually worked themselves into a new perception of patient-therapist relationship.

How does transcending fit into this picture? Psychotherapy views the world from a different perspective than transcending does. Therefore, it emphasizes different aspects of being human. The roots of psychotherapy reach down into the first human nature, that of our physical and psychological selves. Psychotherapy performs an essential service in helping people to resolve the emotional and intellectual conflicts to which our complicated and demanding modern environment exposes them. Existential psychology remains within the same framework as all of psychotherapy — that is, within the confines of the first human nature.

On the other hand, the ability to transcend is a product of the second human nature produced by our creative evolution. It follows that the rationale of transcending differs from the assumptions underlying psychotherapy. To put it simply, psychotherapy focuses on what is best for *me*, while transcending on us, which falls within the framework of idealism. Some authors have proposed that if individuals are better adjusted psychologically, it will have a halo effect which will result in making humanity better. However, unless the adjustment of other people is considered together with one's own, this may prove to be a fallacy.

In some ways this is closer to the thoughts of Martin Buber (1878-1965) a philosopher born in Austria who extended the existential "me" into the concept of *du* — the German word for "thou" in his philosophy of encounter and dialogue. It is hardly surprising that the ability to transcend finds itself at odds with the basic perception of the universe of existentialism. I stated in a preceding chapter that the starting point of transcending is found in idealism. People who transcend do not view their idealism, which gives their life meaning, as self-created. This they would see as analogous to parents who could create their children entirely by their own design without the benefit of their individual genes which make up their inherited human genome. As a parent myself, I would have enormous "existential anxiety" — no, even terror! — in facing such a task and taking responsibility for it. In my book, *Genetic Engineering, Yes, No, or Maybe?* (2000), I explored what such a task would entail. I concluded that with genetic engineering humankind might be deprived of its opportunity to create beyondism. By "beyondism," I mean moving beyond the limitations of gene spreading that biology ascribes to evolution.

Idealism is similar to "morality" in that it can be reduced to simply "not hurting people." This answer was thought to be controversial only because of questions of what "hurting" consists of. It was finally clarified for many people by the coming into existence of a rule which says to treat others as you would like to be treated. Contrary to its critics, that does not mean to treat everyone alike but to relate to others with kindness, understanding, and respect. This is what, ordinarily, all people want. In the same way, "idealism" is basically simple to understand if it is devoid of artificial complications that detract from its central simple meaning which is decency and justice to our fellow human beings. My *Webster New World Dictionary* defines idealism as "behavior or thought based on a conception of things as they should be or as one would wish them to be." This corresponds with the way we have used it in this book. "Wish them to be" is consistent with creative evolution of thought and with the recognition of alternate lifestyles from those under the sway of our first human nature. It represents a behavioral turn-around in human life. It consists of the adoption and use of idealism that creates a fundamental difference between transcending and psychotherapy.

We should also say a few words about meditation and transcending. Transcending like meditation is a lonely experience. Nevertheless those who meditate and those who transcend do not experience loneliness, because, in pursuing their goals, they enter into a bigger picture where loneliness does not exist. Except for this similarity, meditation and transcending differ in their view-of-the-world — their *Weltanschauung* to use the popular name for an all-embracing outlook on life. One might say tentatively that those who seek psychotherapy wish to gain coping ability; those inclined to meditate seek to escape from the tensions and pressures of their life; and those who seek to transcend hope to adopt a world view that will enable them to respond to others with their second human nature. This nature is guided by idealism instead of only by self-preservation.

These generalizations may be attacked as in some ways lacking, because they are admittedly incomplete. However, it serves to highlight the essential points of the distinctions between these three approaches that have a joint endeavor to improve mental health. I do not mean, by any of my statements, to imply that psychiatrists, psychologists, social worker or any other professionals involved with mental health have any less concern for the good of the people of the world as a whole than those who seek to transcend. What I must point out is that those who wish to transcend must make the healthy emotional state of the people of the world one of their primary objectives.

Since the personal peace of mind derived from transcending is a by-product of a new world view, a legitimate question is, "When can humanity be ready for a popular desire to transcend? Must an adherence to idealism occur first?" The answer is that those who wish to transcend must first pass over and beyond self-centeredness. Our first and second natures are interdependent. They not only offer each other the contrast required for awareness of their difference, but they also serve each other as action and reaction. As we have said, psychotherapy caters primarily to our first human nature which we use to look after ourselves. To rise above can only consist of a reaction to something previously in existence which one transcends in order not to perpetuate it. The decision stems from both the desire to be idealistic and the wish to gain peace of mind. The choice of transcending as the means to create peace of mind already implies the presence of this idealism. An attempt to transcend activates our second human nature by itself. Those who choose to transcend should be aware of its alternatives. They must know that these consist of self-enhancement, wealth and social status, and personal power.

By not pursuing these goals and looking for other ways to live, we have already prepared ourselves for the unique experience that transcending provides. That is why simply the desire to transcend, by itself, activates our second human nature. Therefore, as I pointed out in the first chapter of this book, transcending is not confined to saints or the saintly. Any person can enhance his or her life by transcending their negative emotions. In doing so, they assure themselves that they want to make a contribution and use idealism in seeking to enhance their lives.

As I bring this chapter to an end, I wish to point out that it is not biological evolution that, by itself, created the mental life of human beings. Rather, it is something closer to biological *revolution*! That is what creative evolution actually is. Each, in a different way, evolution and revolution, helped to shape transcending's meaning and function. And, as a result of this, we are now closer to being able to rise above ourselves.

CHAPTER ELEVEN

TOPICS FOR DISCUSSIONS

The following topics are presented as questions at the suggestion of some of my professional colleagues. They requested that I include them to provide further opportunity for thoughts or dialogues on transcending. They anticipate that readers may choose to have more clarifications on some topics. The subject matter for discussion is included for this purpose. It does not constitute a formal part of this book.

- You can best transcend things that happen to you or things that have a personal impact. Injustices to others enable you only to feel disgusted. But the impact of the injustice on you, yourself, can be transcended by you.

- Balance: After "He got what was coming to him," balance was restored by way of the courts. Among humans it takes the form of justice — an eye for an eye, a tooth for a tooth. "Restore balance!" may be seen as a human imitation of the action of the cosmos. However, transcending counters this by creating imbalance. This is an aspect of the human revolution against nature. Such phenomena as mud slides and floods are examples of nature's tendency to create balance of the forces which cause order as well as natural disasters on earth that kill people.

- There are three kinds of transcending: 1. Instantaneous, 2. step by step, 3. with struggle. (Note: none of these should be confused with the individual of a species who sacrifices to help the species survive, as in the example of a lone bee sacrificing itself for the beehive.) Idealistic sacrifices for humankind are cognitive, deliberate, and not only caused by instincts alone.

- There are examples of non-recognized transcending in almost every culture. For example, I can hold a plate at a dinner party to help my guests serve themselves first; I hold a door open for them as they enter my house. This is *not* sacrifice or dedication, but a wide-spread custom in which "me first" is rejected without even thinking about it. Is this a form of transcending?

- A common problem is: I can get my mind to transcend but my guts don't follow through. Is this a sign that my two human natures are fighting at the time over which one will guide me?

- It is misleading to think of the universe as all around us. Instead, the universe is within us and all through us. It is more appropriate to think of us as having the universe within ourselves than vice versa. Can we find any reason to support this strange view?

- We have talked of spontaneous transcending. Do you agree with the statement that we should first recognize what we are transcending and why? It also requires some cognition. Unless it is automatic, transcending does not take place with blinders on, or can it do so? Should you be able to experience the mental change from the small picture view of self to a big picture view which includes the significance of human life in the universe?

- It has been stated that in order to transcend, an optimism is necessary which results from the belief that a better world for humankind is possible and desirable. Why should this be necessary?

- A duty to make our world better is not encouraged enough in our schools nor in our homes. Do not confuse this duty with any genetically dictated sacrifices of self to preserve the human genome which may be dictated by our instincts instead of our personal sense of obligation. Where in evolution could such an obligation come from?

- Some people have made transcending into a mystery, and tend to talk about it in hushed tones. Why is that?

- Note: The following has been mentioned in the book before. It is repeated here in somewhat greater detail because it makes a good topic for a discussion.
  It was only after Dr.Koch's death that the monthly, *American Psychologist* (May, 2001) stated on the journal's cover that the main part of this issue was devoted to "One Big Idea: Koch On Psychology." In this issue five psychologists wrote about different aspects of Koch's controversial opinions on the role of psychology. Why didn't he obtain similar credit for his ideas while he was alive?

- Psychotherapy and transcending therapy approach problems of personal adjustment from opposite directions. Psychotherapy attempts to change the individual. Transcending therapy attempts to change the perception of the situation.

Psychology uses insights and realignment of habits to give a person new understanding, a build-up of new self-esteem etc., all of them admittedly worthwhile goals. Transcending therapy, on the other hand, attempts to change behavior by creating an awareness of a person's obligation to his or her human existence. This is achieved by the use of one's second human nature. Today, most cultures in practically all nations tend to obscure this obligation. Why is this?

- I propose an additional twist to the theory of evolution *beyond* natural selection. The universe and life are too complicated to accept the current biological theory of evolution without questioning its single explanation. I see a directional focus in human existence that goes beyond natural selection and represents a need to discover and bring into being what is out there — what is possible. I refer to nature's propensity to actualize the dormant potentialities of the universe. Where, if it exists, does this propensity come from?

- One of these potentialities consists of our second human nature. It does not fit into any category of behavior that our scientists have assigned to natural selection. Some biosociologists have turned and twisted the idea of human goodness to make it fit into natural selection. But they have failed because there is no room for it there. However, there is room for our second human nature in a human creative selection that accompanies natural selection. Where would that "room" originate?

- From earliest times in written history, humans recognized that two different kinds of motivation led to human behavior. One is apparent when we distinguish between behavior that is pleasant, in the sense that it is self-gratifying, and another one deals with a goodness which may exist at the expense of self-gratification. Sometimes we call this "dedication" which comes from the Latin word, to give. Then we say "it is better to give than to receive." How would one apply this to one's own life?

- Humans are capable of acts of great kindness as well as acts of hate, prejudice, and great cruelty. It is an error to think of these extremes as forming a continuum. Instead, one might say, these two kinds of behaviors are on different wave lengths. Most of us recognize the presence of duality within ourselves and in others. According to folk wisdom, some of our feelings arise from "our better nature" or our second nature. Why can't we be satisfied with just one human nature?

- To start with, we face into two directions. Psychotherapy directs us towards self and our personal reactions and behaviors. Transcending points us towards idealism that involves others as well as self. Is this better?

- Transcending is often accompanied by surprises. Sometimes, however, we can be unaware that it has even occurred. When we look back, the picture has changed and the feelings, the event, or the person has changed in the ways we think of them. This goes along with the idea that one's attitude determines our behavior. Where does one's attitude come from?

- Psychotherapy may help dispose you to transcend by clearing your mind of debris that would remove road-blocks to thinking things out. What kind of debris? What kind of road blocks?

- Psychotherapy cannot lead to transcending although it may accompany it. Is this true? If so why?

- Transcending and psychotherapy are opposites in that therapy restores balance while transcendence upsets it. How?

- It is good for us to keep in mind that physicists have found that nothing can be measured without disturbing it. But if we don't understand it, wouldn't it be wise to first measure it to know what it is?

- Transcending is a lonely experience sometimes accompanied by introspection, while therapy is a communal experience with rapport and empathy. Does this differentiate them significantly?

- After transcending, sometimes a new image emerges out of the fog of our modern goals and inhibitions that have taken possession of us. This new image could help us live a new kind of life which would give us peace of mind and happiness. But then wouldn't we be apt to find a new thing to disturb us — tinkering with the human genome for example?

- Merely trying to transcend builds an attitude, and this usually leads to the idealism required for successful transcending. It is not actually transcending but would it help us to do so?

- Another way to conceptualize our first and second natures would be to refer to upper or lower brain centers, and more recently, to structural regions of the brain seen in PET scans of our brains. According to some neuroscientists, they are the seats of our consciousness. More and more we hear about predisposing genetic factors that determine our behavior. Let us not forget that we also have willpower that sometimes can influence genetic expression and that we are also strongly influenced in our behavior by our environment.

- The living world is run by genes, and humans are able to tell some of our genes (but not others) where and how to run, thereby turning the purely biological world upside down. For follow up on this thought read my book, *Genetic Engineering, Yes? No? or Maybe* Minerva Press, London, 2000. You may be surprised by some of the theories in that book and may enjoy discussing them with others.

- Transcendence involves viewing a situation in larger dimensions in order to improve, even if only in the smallest way, the human conditions on earth. This may involve more than a big picture view. It requires the biggest picture view of our personal existence. What could that be? Does the difference in what is viewed explain the different opinions we have?

- Reason gets in the way of itself when we search for it where there is none. Transcending doesn't have that problem. Can you think of why this may be so?

- Modern cognitive therapy consists of many intellectual processes combined to produce willed action. We can give cognitive therapy to ourselves by reviewing what, in our life, has worked for us and what has failed to do so.

- In therapy we may learn how to cope with injustice, hurts, slights, and even with hate directed against us. In transcending we do not even try to deal with these. We do not ignore nor deny the occurrence of such events. Instead we jump over them and they will be out of our sight. Then we do not have to react to them on a personal basis. By not responding to them we tend to discourage their having an enduring existence. The point is that we try not to perpetuate them. That you do not do so solely is not only for your own sake, but for the good of humankind as well. Why?

- Oddly, revenge and transcendence have a basic element in common. It is to get a hateful event over with and help stamp it out of a person's mind. What disadvantages are there in this?

- In contrast to psychotherapy which restores balance, transcending creates imbalance —"not getting even, not seeking revenge, nor retribution." To obtain revenge is a powerful urge absorbed from the nature of the laws of the universe. Love, in return for hate; and walking the extra mile as Jesus recommended, promote imbalance. This is a remarkable capability of humans — totally unnatural, and even antinatural—and represents a twist in the evolution of life. Nature always restores balance over time in the physical world. What would our doing so entail?

- Psychotherapy enables one to forgive by recognizing the origins and influences that precipitated an act. Transcending does not require that recognition. Can you think of the reason for this oddity of transcending?

- Here are ways to handle obstacles. First, by prevention; next by cognition, that is, seeing the obstacle rationally with understanding. This is often enough to be able to solve a problem but in some cases it may not be so. Example, the new member of the social club did not respond in a friendly manner to the hostess who had invited him. Her feelings were deeply hurt.

Later someone told her that he had ordered new hearing aids which as yet had not been delivered. The reason why he failed to respond was that he was unable to hear the hostess. Many times we get angry when we do not know the whole story. Transcending cures this *before* it happens because the new member's lack of acknowledgment would not have been a source of anger for the hostess. Perhaps she would have thought, as we often do in transcending, his lack of response really is not that important to me or to the social club. The big picture might have been that, because of his past accomplishments, he would be a desirable person to have as a member. What can we learn from this?

- To view the big picture view, one must know where to look and what to look for. The Biggest Picture always would include the whole universe and its cosmic potentialities. How can one view it, comprehend it, feel in touch with it? Some would say by achieving Nirvana. Others would chose using one's own individual mind to attain maximum self-actualization.

- In spite of our great similarities to other animals, humans differ from them, not only in cognition, but in our potentiality for self-actualization. The human essence is not a straight line of a continuum from the animal world in which we are rooted. The difference is not *evolution but revolution* which is the human way. Paleontologists now know that what formerly was thought of as a steady evolutionary change was a mistaken notion when applied to situations including the acquisition of our human nature. Where did it come from? (For the answer, see the Postscript.)

- We see our human nature in our capacity for infinite love and also in the capacity for infinite cruelty to fellow members of our species. Few other creatures are as capable. Both capabilities are necessary to allow us the largest possible amount of free choice.

- Transcending is not a cure-all when alternatives are more appropriate, — for example, in having righteous anger at injustice, or resistance to bad ideas.

- Does one have to *overcome* or *transcend* prejudice? Is it correct to say that the nature of prejudice generally makes it more suitable for overcoming? It depends on the type of prejudice that we are dealing with. Some types can be transcended while others, in which dehumanizing takes place, can not be transcended. Why? Because this acts only on the smallest picture. Are there other reasons?

- The concept that something is not really important is also used as a therapeutic tool in cognitive therapy, where a person is taught to challenge his "faulty" belief systems.

- In contrast to psychotherapy, mini-transcending includes some ethical dimension that is "doing something not only because it makes one feel better, but because it is consistent with one's idealism."

- In our daily lives, we transcend in ways that we are not aware of, for example, when transported beyond ourselves when we listen to music.

- Mini-transcending implies having a view of a larger picture.

- "It is not important" just happens to be one of the most important statements that a person can make.

- How do knowledge and human imagination support each other to produce creative evolution? What do you think Albert Einstein meant when he said that imagination is more important than knowledge?

- Temporary transcendence is certainly possible. Sometimes we think that we have surmounted a particular problem, only to find in a subsequent occasion, that it still, or again, is a problem. Is this very discouraging?

- You don't want to divest yourself of all hostility, even if this were possible. However, you may wish to override those angers that are of no consequence in the long run. They merely cause angry reactions in return. Principles that violate morality, such as injustice to others, do call for anger and outspoken disapproval. Transcending doesn't mean that you shouldn't speak up when it is appropriate. Remember that, occasionally, your first human nature still has a legitimate role in your life.

Postscript

The Origin of Human Goodness

I was invited to participate in a critique devoted to Darwin's theory of evolution in our local newspaper, the Ventura City Star. In my comments I suggested that a development took place in human evolution which seemed to contradict one of evolution's major tenets. I referred to the belief that only those mutational changes were maintained in living organisms which conformed to the demands of natural selection. Evolutionists do not accept any alternative explanation for the long term alterations in species including our own. The following quotation from Harvard professor emeritus, Edward O. Wilson, will help to lead up to my point of view: (From his book, *Naturalist* (1994),

> Evolution seemed firmly grounded in genetics, at least to the following extent: nothing the geneticists could say ... seemed likely to overturn the modern synthesis (which is that only natural selection is a factor in evolution). Only a complete surprise, something major and out of the blue, could accomplish that. To this day nothing so radical has occurred.

I suggest that such a "surprise" did occur. It hinged on the fact that when *mixed in a unique way,* once in a great while the mixture may produce something new which differs greatly from its original components. Usually, the ingredients of the mixture must be present in the precise proportions needed to cause such a change. The change in classical evolution leading to human morality was, apparently, brought about by natural selection itself considering the fact I mentioned. Illustrations of similar transformations are found in many fields of science including the human sciences. However, the clearest example of this phenomenon occurs in chemistry. For example, hydrogen reacts with oxygen to produce a new substance — water.

I do not try to equate evolution with chemistry. I have turned to chemistry in this case only to provide a clear example of the fact that if the laws of the cosmos permit it, any mixture of ingredients may sometimes produce an entirely new product. That is how some of the variations in living species took place. When certain ingredients about 3 ½ billion years ago combined with other substances, the mixture of components produced simple forms of life. Life was able to replicate itself in specific ways to produce additional life. First this occurred by the division of mother cells which produced identical daughter cells.

Subsequently, a remarkable improvement occurred when males contributed semen which caused greater variation in the offsprings of many living things. Biological evolution, by itself, could not have anticipated such a change. It could only anticipate the kinds of things occurring when it was observed that they occurred.

All the difference in forms of life were ascribed by Darwin to the occasional mistakes that nature makes when it replicates genes. Most of these mistakes caused organisms to become extinct. Only those mistakes that were beneficial to spreading genes, under the condition of the times, were perpetuated. Most of these caused small changes that eventually created different species and variations within species. This is how some organisms gained complexity, and many new species evolved through natural selection. Among them probably were the order of primates which had developed large brains relative to their total body weight, and opposable thumbs for grasping objects.

We are classified as primates. In human life, there is a near identity of our genome with that of chimpanzees. However, there are also important differences. It demonstrates that genes alone do not account for everything in life, particularly in human life. Among our differences with apes is our human mixture of cerebral characteristics, especially those most susceptible to the influences of our social environment. Also, we have the ability to visualize immaterial properties which lead to perceptions no other living creature can make. One of these perceptions combined with our imagination and led to what we call "human values," that are accepted for their own worth rather than solely for biological advantages. The 18th century German philosopher, Immanuel Kant, maintained that genuine morality cannot have any ulterior motives. It must exist only in order to exist as ethics, justice, compassion, kindness, and so on, whether there are, or are not, any biological or genetic gains.

Let us assume that evolution produced the kind of morality that Kant called genuine; that is, that it existed without having an ulterior motive. Unlike reciprocal morality and other moralities with self-centered goals, a morality without biological gains would be something spectacularly new in evolution if it persisted. Like many other genetic "mistakes" that occur in nature, we would expect such a morality to be cast off in time if it did not help us meet the demands of natural selection. However, humans have the mental resources necessary to incorporate such a "mistake" into our lifestyles. Therefore these values could exist even though they might sometimes present a handicap to our survival. At this point we must examine the problem of logic that is involved in my opinion.

The following quotation from the book, *Taking Darwin Seriously* by Michael Ruse, professor at the University of Guelph (Ontario) reveals this problem:

How can you possibly get values from something (evolution) that says that the building blocks of nature are blind, random variations? Darwinism says you could as well have one organic state as another. The point about values is that you are dealing with standards. You are talking about things on an absolute scale. Is it wrong? Is it good? Is it bad? Without progress (he means, the existence of progress and the changes caused by progress) the search for morality vanishes. And Darwinism denies progress.

However, in time, "progress" could occur by "blind chance" among human beings (unless evolution is seen as also progressive) through a mixture of new genetic traits combined with enhanced social environments. What would such a mixture consist of? Among other possibilities are the long period of dependency as neonates, an ability for making a high level of abstractions, and a far-reaching, innovative imagination. When these were combined they could have produced a Kantian type of morality. This kind of a morality permitted us to select and maintain certain behaviors for their inherent qualities without necessarily requiring them to contribute to the survival of our gene pool.

The coexistence of the ability to spread genes and at the same time to preserve a morality maintained for its own sake, will not cause our extinction. We will not inevitably die if we occasionally eat chocolate bars with high sugar content and lots of cholesterol. If we have compensating survival skills and health habits that outweigh the survival disadvantages created by our adoption of a Kantian morality, we need not become extinct.

Some scientists believe that there is no such thing as a Kantian morality. Their minds visualize only a pure and uncontaminated "struggle for existence." They ascribe everything that is human to it. It takes time and open-mindedness for an innovation like a Kantian morality to become noticeable, especially when there are many other behaviors that appear like them.

We are a relatively new species in terms of length of life on earth. Up to this time we have given the Kantian morality mostly lip-service which makes it insincere and difficult to recognize, but demonstrates our awareness of its existence. A morality that exists solely for personal gain and to spread our genes is easier to conceptualize. Since it is older it makes more "sense" to people like us, who were raised on the exploitation often seen in nature and human nature. Perhaps we must look to future millennia before it becomes a pronounced human characteristic. I suggest that a start in that direction has been made by our ability to transcend. Let us define some terms that are used in this book.

SUMMARY

What is bad? To gain satisfaction from hurting other people, or indifference to their suffering or worse, to take advantage of their plight. What is good? Impulses, desires, intentions to assist people and other living things that are not dangerous to humans. "Bad" and "Good" in this sense are not opposites as they seem to be but they are, nevertheless, worlds apart since they have different functions and results. Badness is comparable to entropy which by its definition creates ever greater disorder in the universe. Goodness represents the creative forces in the universe and contributes to its overarching beauty that inspires wonder and awe. These are definitions that are admittedly slanted towards human beings but this is logical since this is what we happen to be. We certainly wouldn't be expected to postulate definitions that would center on the well-being of microbes that are dangerous to humankind, although in one sense, they have an equal right to exist as we have.

Possession of even a trace of independence from natural selection caused humans to differ, perhaps, imperceptibly, but intrinsically, from most other forms of life and to differ from them on the side of goodness. In order to explain how this might happen, I have offered a mechanism to account for the concept that the proliferation of genes and "survival of the fittest," need not be the sole characteristic of human life.

In the future, natural selection may be accompanied or replaced by moral selection. Then we will at last create the condition on earth for which we have longed ever since we became true human beings.

BIBLIOGRAPHY

Batson, C. D. & Thompson, E. R. (April 2001) Chapter 8, *Current Directions In Psychological Science.*

Behe, M. J. (1996) *Darwin's Black Box.* New York: Touchstone, Simon & Schuster, Inc.

Bergson, Henri (1911) *Creative Evolution.* New York: Holt.

Foley, R. (1997) *Humans Before Humanity.* Malden. MA: Blackwell Publishers Inc.

Huxley, J. S. (1942) *Evolution: The Modern Synthesis.* London: Allen and Unwin.

Johnson, R. E.(1975) *In Quest Of A New Psychology.* New York: Human Science Press.

Kelly, W. L. & Tallon, A (1967) *Readings In The Philosophy Of Man.* New York: McGraw-Hill, Inc.

Kent, T. C. (1987) *A Psychologist Answers Your Questions.* Bryn Mawr, PA: Dorrance & Co.

Kent, T. C. (2000) *Genetic Engineering — Yes, No or Maybe?* London: Minerva Press.

Kent, T. C. (1995) *Mapping The Human Genome.* Lanham, MD: University Press Of America, Inc.

Kent, T. C. (1995) *Poems For Living.* San Diego: Human Sciences Center Press.

Menninger, Karl (1942) *Love Against Hate.* New York: Harcourt, Brace.

Ruse, Michael, (1998) *Taking Darwin Seriously.* Amherst, NY: Prometheus Books.

Satre, J. P. (1962) *Sketch For A Theory Of Emotions*, trans. P. Mairet, London: Methuen.

Wilson, E. O. (1994) *Naturalist.* Washington, D.C.: Island Press/Shearwater Books.

INDEX

Note: Some entries that appear throughout the book, such as, transcend, psychotherapy, and first and second human natures are not listed in the index, except for their initial definitions.

A

abstraction, 67
acupuncturists, 53
Adam and Eve, 62
adrenalin, 20
African-American, 26
aging, disabilities associated with, 52
aloneness, 98, 101
American Autoimmune Related Diseases Organization, 58
Aristophanes, 7
Aristotle, 12
Aryan Brothers, 87

B

balance, 103
behavior,
    antisocial, 90
    maladjusted (neuroses), 96-97
behavioral analysis, 97
behavioral science, 4, 61, 77
Batson, C. Daniel, 76

Bergson, Henri, 81
beyond, 8-9, 17, 22, 28-29, 42, 51, 58-60, 95, 106
"beyondism," 100
Big Bang, 73
big picture, 3-4, 8, 27-28, 31-32, 43, 47, 56-57, 111
biofeedback, 52
Boys Club, 29
braincenter, lower or upper, 3, 89, 108
Buber, Martin, 99
Buddha, 14, 24

C

Cardyceps, fungus species, 71
cataract surgery, 31
catharsis, 33-34
cerebral cortex, 3, 48, 63
chiropractors, 53
civilization, 2
client-therapist relationship, 99
cloning, 13
common sense, 4

D

Darwin, 70-71, 94, 116
Darwinism, modern, 66, 118
death, 58-60
dehumanizing, 13, 63, 86, 88, 112
"deliberate, salutary absentmindedness," 36
Devil, 62-64
divorce, 41-43
drugs, mind altering, 6

E

ego defenses, 44
Einstein, Albert, 55, 74, 113
Emerson, Ralph Waldo, 12, 44
emotions, negative and angry, 1
evil, 65-67
evolution,
    biological, 48, 65, 70, 116
    creative, 5-6, 47-48, 57, 69-70, 75, 81, 93, 99, 102
    natural selection, 70, 73, 106, 115-116, 120
existentialism, 98-99

F

Fletcher, Jack M., 84
Freud, Sigmund, 5, 71

G

Gandhi, 24
genetic engineering, 13, 24, 66, 73, 100, 109
Genetic Engineering, Yes, No, or Maybe? 66, 100
Genghis Khan, 85
God, 25, 27-28, 37, 55, 62, 85
good judgment, 3
goodness, 55, 65-67, 70-79, 82-85, 92-94, 106-107, 119-120

H

Hebrew Bible, 62, 72
higher self, 3
Hinduism, 91
Homo sapiens sapiens, 48, 72, 81-82, 94
human behavior, current, 2
human brutality, 5
human genome, inherited, 100, 108
humankind, 4, 65, 85, 87
Humanistic, 2, 4
humanity, 6
human nature, 3-6, 15-18, 20-22, 25-26, 29, 43, 47, 52, 65, 71-72, 75-76, 78, 92, 94, 99, 102, 106, 108
    first human nature, definition of, 15
    second human nature, definition of, 15
Huxley, Thomas Henry, 82
hypnotherapy, 53
hypnosis, 52-53
hypocrisy, 76

I

idealism, 3-6, 12, 19, 22-23, 26-28, 42-46, 81, 88, 94, 99-102, 108, 112
imagination, 52, 55, 72, 74, 83, 87-88, 113
imaging, 97
inspiration, 12

J

James, William, 37
Jesus, 20, 24, 110
Johnson, Richard E., 1
Judeo Christian Religion, 62

K

Kansas, University of, 76
Kant, Immanuel, 74, 117
Kantian morality, 118-119
Kierkegaard, Soren, 98
King, Martin Luther, 24
Kipling, Rudyard, 89-90
Koch, Sigmund, 2, 105

L

Lao Tze, 24
La Rochefoucauld, Francois, 76
Lucifer, 64

M

Marcus, Steven, 89
Mason, Paul, 89
meaning, double, 31, 34
meditation, 1, 6, 97, 101
Menninger Clinic, 2
Menninger, Karl, 2, 4, 6, 92
morality, 113, 117-119
mysticism, 1
mythology, 72
    Babylonian, 64
    Chaldean, 64
    Egyptian, 64
    Zoroastrian, 64

N

natural selection, 70, 73, 106, 115-116, 120
negative and angry emotions, 1, 36
neurotransmitters, 63
New York University, 65
Nietzsche, 24
nirvana, 91, 111

P

pain, 51-58,
    as punishment, 52
    chronic, 51-52, 54, 56-58
    emotional, 51
    inability to feel, 51
    management, 56
    mental, 51-52, 58
    physical, 51-52, 58
    psychosomatic, 54
painful experiences, 1
peace of mind, 39, 79, 87, 91
PET brain scans, 84, 108
Plato, 98
Poems for Living, 45-46, 59-60
possibility, 85
post-traumatic injuries, 52
potentiality, 6, 65, 73, 84-85, 93, 106, 111
prayer, 55
pre-frontal cortex, 3, 48
psychoanalysis, 96
psychodrama, 97
psychological perception, 21
A Psychologist Answers Your Questions, 3
psychology, 1-2, 72
psychoses (mental illness), 94-96

R

Regina, Canada, University of, 1
religions, 91
retirement, 77-78

Revelations, Book of, 13
revenge, 21, 23, 110
revolution, biological, 102
Rousseau, Jean Jacques, 78
Ruse, Michael, 117

S

Sartre, Jean Paul, 98
Schweitzer, Albert, 24
self-preservation, 101
serotonin, 63
Southern Colorado, University of, 37
spirituality, 72
sublimation, 98
superego, 72
symbiosis, 70-71

T

T therapy, 44
Taoism, 91
teenagers, antisocial, 77, 87, 90
temptation, 60-64
Texas, University of, 84
therapy,
    cognitive, 44, 97, 109, 112
    group, 56, 96
    paradoxical, 97
    release, 97

transcending, 3, 44-45
Thompson, Elizabeth R., 76
Thoreau, Henry David, 5, 43
transcend, definition of, 12
transcendent, 12
transcendental, 12
transcendental meditation, 12, 97
Tutu, Bishop, 79, 85, 87-88

U

uniqueness, awareness of one's own, 98
universal ethics, 98

V

vegetarians, 89

W

Weinberger, Joel, PhD, 36
Weltanschauung, 101
Wilson, Edward O., 115, 118
witness, expert in criminal trials, 62

Y

yoga, 6

DÉJÀ PARU

Derek Van Arman

IL

Traduit de l'anglais (États-Unis) par Johan-Frédérik Hel Guedj

Le chef-d'oeuvre inconnu du roman de serial killer.

Les très grands romans de serial killer se comptent sur les doigts d'une main : *Le Dahlia noir*, de James Ellroy, *Le Silence des agneaux*, de Thomas Harris, *Le Poète*, de Michael Connelly. Après *Au-delà du mal*, de Shane Stevens, nous sommes heureux de vous proposer un nouveau sommet du genre, *IL*, de Derek Van Arman.

« La plupart des tueurs en série n'ont rien à voir avec les mythes qu'ils ont engendrés. Ils ne vivent pas isolés, au milieu des bois ou au fin fond d'un asile. Ce sont vos propres voisins. Comme Bundy, Statler et des centaines d'autres, ce sont des individus que vous croisez aux réunions de parents d'élèves ou aux matchs de base-ball, ils prennent le bus avec vous, leurs enfants jouent avec les vôtres et ils récitent peut-être même le Notre-Père avec vous, lors de vos réunions de famille. » Ainsi parle Jack Scott, directeur de l'agence fédérale en charge des crimes violents et spécialiste des serial killers. Lorsqu'une mère et ses deux filles sont sauvagement assassinées dans une mise en scène macabre, Jack, qui pensait avoir tout enduré, va entreprendre la chasse à l'homme la plus délicate, et la plus perverse, de sa longue carrière.

Roman choral, baroque, d'une ampleur peu commune, *Il* marque d'une pierre noire l'histoire du roman de serial killer. Cette descente vers le mal, angoissante et crépusculaire, au suspense implacable, nous donne un aperçu d'un réalisme rare sur les méthodes d'investigation de la police américaine. À tel point que l'auteur a été mis en examen par le FBI afin qu'il livre les sources lui ayant permis d'être aussi proche de la réalité. Problèmes judiciaires qui expliquent pourquoi ce livre, paru aux États-Unis en 1992 et immédiatement devenu culte, est resté inédit en France jusqu'à ce jour.

Derek Van Arman est un pseudonyme. IL est son seul roman.

À PARAÎTRE

Avril 2013

Penny Hancock
Désordre

Traduit de l'anglais par Julie Sibony

Après *Les Visages* de Jesse Kellerman,
après *Avant d'aller dormir* de S. J. Watson,
après *Les Apparences* de Gillian Flynn,
la nouvelle découverte Sonatine.

Sonia, la quarantaine, mène une vie confortable dans la jolie maison des bords de la Tamise où elle a grandi. Mais depuis que son mari, Greg, multiplie les déplacements professionnels à l'étranger et que leur fille Kit est partie à l'université, son existence lui pèse. Alors que Greg la presse de quitter Londres pour se rapprocher de lui, Sonia se sent incapable de quitter sa maison, décor d'une jeunesse pour laquelle elle éprouve la plus vive nostalgie. À l'heure du bilan, elle réalise en effet que son adolescence a été le seul moment vraiment heureux de son existence, celui où les émois et les sentiments ont été les plus forts et les plus purs. Aussi, lorsque Jez, 15 ans, le neveu d'une de ses amies, Helen, vient frapper à sa porte pour emprunter un disque, Sonia, prise d'une pulsion inexplicable, décide de ne plus le laisser partir. Elle se met alors à nourrir une étrange et inquiétante obsession pour la jeunesse de Jez, qu'elle tient séquestré. Lorsque Helen signale la disparition du jeune garçon à la police, une enquête minutieuse commence, qui ne tarde pas à s'orienter vers un suspect inattendu. À travers ce récit conjuguant les voix de Sonia et d'Helen, Penny Hancock nous offre un portrait magnifique de deux femmes à un carrefour de leur vie, aux prises avec leurs peurs et leurs faiblesses, leurs secrets et leurs solitudes. Surtout, elle nous donne un roman où règne une tension extrême, une terrifiante histoire de folie, cruellement humaine, qui culmine dans un suspense infernal, digne du légendaire *Misery*, de Stephen King.

Penny Hancock vit à Londres. *Désordre* est son premier roman.

À PARAÎTRE

Mai 2013

Hilary Mantel

Le Conseiller 1 – Dans l'ombre des Tudor

Traduit de l'anglais par Fabrice Pointeau

Dans la lignée des *Tudor*, le premier roman événement d'une trilogie qui a enflammé l'Europe et les États-Unis. Les fans de roman historique vont hurler de plaisir !

Angleterre, 1520. Règne des Tudor. Le roi Henri VIII n'a pas de fils pour lui succéder. Situation préoccupante qui pourrait entraîner le pays sur le chemin de la guerre civile. Aussi décide-t-il de divorcer de Catherine d'Aragon, avec qui il est marié depuis plus de vingt ans, pour épouser Anne Boleyn, dont il est tombé amoureux. Son conseiller, le cardinal Wolsey, échouant à obtenir l'accord du pape, un jeune homme plein de fougue et de ressources va peu à peu entrer dans les bonnes grâces du roi et l'aider à vaincre l'opposition en provoquant un schisme avec Rome. Son nom : Thomas Cromwell. Ambitieux, idéaliste et opportuniste à la fois, fin politicien et manipulateur-né, celui-ci est au début d'une carrière qui va modifier profondément et durablement le visage du royaume.

Avec *Le Conseiller*, lauréat du Booker Prize et salué dans le monde entier par une critique unanime, Hilary Mantel nous propose un fabuleux voyage au cœur d'une société en plein bouleversement. Prenant pour sujet l'une de ces périodes clés de notre civilisation où l'histoire, la politique, les passions et les destinées individuelles se confondent, elle nous livre un portrait sans précédent de la maison Tudor.

Hilary Mantel est née en 1952. Le Conseiller *est le premier volet d'une trilogie consacrée à la maison Tudor. Sonatine publiera en 2014 et 2015 les deux opus suivants.*

Mis en pages par Soft Office – Eybens (38)
Imprimé en France par CPI Bussière
à Saint-Amand-Montrond (Cher)
N° d'édition : 177 – N° d'impression : 124337/4.
Dépôt légal : mars 2013.
ISBN 978-2-35584-177-4